Mick made the 'very simple decision' to completely change his professional focus eight years ago to predominantly work with children with behavioural issues following a long and successful career in high-end house design, project management and 5* commercial interior fit-out – post being forced to retire from professional football aged 19 through injury. He and his wife, Sian, have been foster carers with an ethical not-for-profit agency since 2006 and in January 2017, they designed and 'self-built' their own family home, completing the project in only 22 weeks. After joining their families in 2002, they turned towards caring for others, feel blessed and wish to share their strategies with all of you working with children.

Dedicated to Sian, who lights the pathway for so many and without whom, I would not have started or continued to experience this amazing journey.

Mick Jewell

Are Difficult Children Difficult, or Just Different? What if We Can Change to Help Them?

AUSTIN MACAULEY PUBLISHERS™

LONDON · CAMBRIDGE · NEW YORK · SHARJAH

A CIP catalogue record for this title is available from the British Library.

ISBN 9781528915694 (Paperback)
ISBN 9781528961349 (ePub e-book)

www.austinmacauley.com

First Published (2019)
Austin Macauley Publishers Ltd
25 Canada Square
Canary Wharf
London
E14 5LQ

Ellis and Owen (Ted) Jewell, my sons, who are amazing young men and have been, since they were very young, accepting others and their very different ways, traits, habits, behaviours and being so flexible and thoughtful.

Lauren, Tom and Robbie Dance, my step-children, who taught me 'the ropes' of looking after someone else's children, changing my approach and 'angles'.

The Foster Care Cooperative established by the great man that will always be Laurie Gregory, and specifically Helen Underwood for taking the risk on Sian and me becoming Foster Carers.

Wade Reeve, Rachel Robertson, Maggie Brennan, Mlu Mbambo, Lucy Mason and B, R, D and S, who have allowed Sian and me to make many mistakes whilst getting to know their very unique ways and needs – you are all amazing and must always believe that.

Gloria Armistead and Susan Fleisher, who promoted the caring aspects of FASD in Fasaware and NOFAS UK respectively – I learned so much from them and was proud to assist where I could in speaking and teaching roles.

Malcolm Baker, a truly amazing SENCO, who understood the need to be flexible in an educational setting and put it into practice, achieving spectacular and quite honestly, 'unbelievable' results. He taught me so much about Education settings and had the time to discuss and trial the ideas that we believed 'could' work.

All of the professionals Sian and I have worked with along the way in Schools, Virtual Schools, Social Work, Fostering Agencies, Local Authorities, CAMH, FASD support groups, Coram BAAF, Guardians, Advocates, etc. – if I mentioned you all, we would have a whole new book.

All of the other Foster Carers, Adopters, Birth Parents, Child Minders, Grandparents, extended family members and siblings that I have been lucky enough to work alongside and gain knowledge, strategies, skills and strength from.

Thank you and I hope you all continue the great work you do with a huge smile and lots of joy.

Table of Contents

Introduction

Can we label a child with a mental health or behavioural label that 'sticks', never 'falls off' and never needs editing or altering?

The simple answer is 'no' or at best, 'not in most cases'. Children start at different points, naturally have somewhere in the region of a billion neurons waiting to step into action, process differently, mature at differing paces and then we throw in 'real life', family, early life pathways, and a million and one external influences just to 'mix it all up'. Why do we expect all children will react to the 'traditional' parenting and teaching methods, and not assess each individual, treating them as an 'individual'?

Why do we label children – especially in care or in vulnerable or confusing situations – and then attempt to send them down the same reparative single path, and expect we can change them without changing our methods?

Why does Society expect us all to be the same at a certain age, school year or transitional stage and then desperately try to find reasons why we have not met these expectations? We often blame that, label it, and then create even more barriers and even less opportunities for that young person to thrive and blossom in their own time – each individual's traits and skills are a 'gateway to progression' and we must try harder to understand where this young person is at, fits in and best functions, not just say 'because they are 8, they can only work with other 8 year olds'.

The intention of this book is to open our minds, accept every child is an individual, and as carers, teachers, social workers and all professionals working with children, use this book as a single point of reference or discussion to raise the questions, identify the skills, find the gaps and start to work together – at the youngest possible age – to bridge the gaps, boost the skills, keep raising the questions and trial differing strategies with no fear of failure. In turn, we will promote improved behaviours, learning progression, confidence, self-esteem, positive strategies and most importantly of all, individuality.

There is no hard and fast learning style that can be confirmed as 'the code' to every individual brain or that defines and works for every child. It is the responsibility of the network of adults that surround each child to ensure we work closely together to do our best to work out the 'current code' for that child, set an individual program and work with them to improve their outcome. This 'code' will change at many points, but we need to be more flexible, and allow differing strategies to be tried, tested and progressed, or quite simply shelved if they do not work for that individual. The important element is that we do not shy away from trying as many differing strategies as are necessary and that we are not fearful of failure. It is important that we do not forget that Humans learn from mistakes, and that if we assess, evaluate and monitor, we will succeed and learn.

Chapter 1
The Definition of Strategy

Success for any individual involves introducing, building, trialling, failing and forging strategies that improve the current situation. It is important that we want to build individuals not suppress talent and skill in favour of working to the current 'supposedly tried and tested' parenting, educational and progressive working models.

We are learning about the human brain and behaviours every day, and we read more and more about individuals who have succeeded against all the odds living with Bi-Polar, Personality disorders, autism, Foetal Alcohol Spectrum Disorder, Abusive backgrounds, Dyslexia and many more individual human or lifestyle conditions that if we are fearful of, halt progress, and if we embrace, often produce very special people. Very often these individuals did not have labels at a young age, they were just different, or if they did have labels, they were very often incorrect and altered along the way – many times in some cases.

Many elements of individuality are recognised by obvious behaviours in the child, but many are missed, ignored, misunderstood or sometimes even tagged 'they'll grow out of it'. Many items can seem minor but when put together, cause a much larger distraction to learning, progressing and generally, feeling balanced – we must feel comfortable and prepared to progress. Such items as diet, timing, clothing, aromas, lighting, the length of the task, the environment, the sound, the position, the distractions and basically, any variable can throw any individual off balance, enough to create a barrier to learning and progressing. Later in the book, we discuss many example case studies and situations that you may have already experienced with individuals, and I am sure you have many more of your own that you are able to cite – and hopefully, share with everyone on our blog forum @........

One example that sticks in my mind is an 11 year old young person that struggled at school and felt vulnerable as they had missed over 50% of school by the point that they entered a new foster placement. Upon early discussion with the network of teaching staff at an excellent, forward thinking mainstream secondary school, it was put to the table by the Maths teacher – a very experienced individual – that 'they cannot cope in my lesson on Wednesdays, but they are a delight on Fridays and it is like I have two different identical twins that attend my classes alternately'. When asked to add more detail it came to light that Wednesday's lesson was positioned in the same classroom as Friday lessons, with the same pupils, the same teacher and the same chair for that person, but they were very unsettled, could not learn, and behaved appallingly. The only identified variable being the time of the lesson 'perhaps, it because they know it is Friday and feel they can wee the end of the learning week, which can be very tiring for someone who is catching up and has the anxieties associated with being in care, not many friends etc. etc.?'. Upon further discussion, it was identified that Wednesdays lesson takes place at 11.30am and Friday lesson is at 1.30pm, where the carer then interjected and offered the possibility that the young person was simply hungry, and had been known to suffer with varying blood sugar levels that increase anxiety and panic after spending long periods without food in their younger years. It was a suggestion that was then put to the other teachers who taught the young person at that period each day during the week and they all confirmed the same appraisal as the Maths teacher, who, thankfully, saw the young person twice a week so was able to not label them as 'a problem'. The strategy was to offer that child a digestive biscuit at 11.15am break time each day – and not rely on them to hold and manage, as it would be eaten at the incorrect time – to see if this helped.

The outcome – no crime was committed with the biscuit between lessons. The young person's learning improved significantly, not only in Maths, but in all lessons. This very simple but effective strategy also improved the week of, at least, five members of staff and somewhere in the region of 150 students, who did not have to witness the disruption, and lose much of their lesson and subsequent learning time. It also improved the social outcome for the young person as they were much more friendly and relaxed. A tiny amount of individual intervention made a huge impact on not only that young person but many others.

A strategy is much like a label – it can be short lived, long term, progressive, moveable, temporary, trialled, repetitive, revisited, dropped, assessed, reassessed, tweaked and also can be completely wrong. It is very often not recognised and cannot be simplified or attached in a negative form, thus being enormously more positive than a label, and in most cases, unable to judge someone by, switch off to them or be prejudiced towards them.

Never be afraid to make mistakes or changes. Do not be risk averse.

In the following sections of this book, we will discover that individuals come in extremes and extreme strategies can be trialled, however, sometimes, it's the simple things that balance the individual. We will not cover all instances and examples, but we will promote discussion and confidence in being flexible and forward thinking, along with communication and teamwork.

Chapter 2
Behaviours

Are the children you care for, work with, teach, have adopted or have input into in any form showing any of the behaviours as listed on the opposite page (some are age specific but where possible they cover age 4 up to age 17)? We have inserted a tick box blank worksheet for you to remove and copy/add more than one child's traits and behaviours. You can keep, and update for each individual to assess progress and development:-

- Difficulties with processing SIMPLE instructions
- Easily distracted
- Is defiant or refuses completely to conform
- Rarely follows through on instructions
- Very often interrupts/intrudes – struggles to listen
- Never consider the consequences before engaging
- Has difficulties in organising tasks and activities for self
- Finds transitions and change stressful
- Displays an odd or inconsistent sleep pattern
- Finds it difficult to make or maintain eye contact
- Is not very cuddly
- Tells lies about the obvious
- Lies when it would be easier to tell the truth
- Wants the last word
- Uses incessant chatter as a regular habit
- Shows an increase or delayed startle response
- Has problems with social interactions

- Struggles with a speech and language – communication
- Is over responsive to stimuli
- Is under responsive to stimuli
- Is very inflexible and displays stubbornness
- Shows difficulty seeing cause and effect
- Struggles with relationship and has problems sharing
- Poor recognition of time and its concept
- Struggles with poor money recognition and management
- Has receptive issues with information processing
- Seems good at talking but it is mainly scripted
- Often has tantrums, loses temper, cries or shouts
- Argues with adults
- Answers 'I don't know' to most simple questions
- Mouths or mimics words that you say – echolalia
- Blames others for their mistakes
- Is easily annoyed by others
- Is oversensitive to noise and/or smells
- Cannot taste food correctly
- Cannot concentrate or focus on a task for long
- Has obvious memory issues
- Has unusual responses to pain
- Displays excessive shame when wrong

We will be attempting to discuss and offer strategies to cover most of the behaviours identified and listed in the table, and will progress the list and it's definitions in terms of overall strategies and living conditions, teaching environments, and in general, 'balanced' terms.

It is very possible that the child showing a number of elements from the list of behaviours could be/have been affected by a number of issues. These could have been experienced recently, at a younger age, knowingly, unconsciously and in many instances, 'in utero'. We will discuss and detail the difficulties that a child may have endured in greater detail later in the book, and will summarise, not diagnose, the possible areas that may have been or could still be affected, thus identifying future strategies, and maybe, in some instances, moving towards necessary labels via diagnoses from the relevant and skilled professionals. It is very important at this stage that we do not concentrate on attempting to diagnose – we are not looking to label. We are looking to correctly identify behaviours and implement/trial strategies that will improve the current difficulties.

Let's build a picture over time, and include information from everyone who works with and around the child, sometimes even siblings, peers or other children in care within the same family can have input, and be very influential in allowing the young person to reflect and understand, whilst not feeling alone or isolated. We must constantly monitor, assess and evaluate each behaviour that the young person is displaying, exploring, using, is unable to understand, is unable to alter or is having difficulty with. The child in question may be able to eventually take ownership of the behaviour, understand it, and build and evaluate strategies, but this is a skilled intervention that takes time, trust, maturity and full understanding. Later in the book, we discuss the potential timings, location, acceptance, and finer points that need to be carefully considered and evaluated prior to this point.

We cannot wait until the modern medical world find solutions to the many brain based issues that humans experience, and quite honestly, if they do find solutions it would not be ethical to use them on children and many question the use of behavioural enhancing/diminishing drugs, labelling them as 'dampening' and 'non-progressive'.

It is much more beneficial to, where possible, resolve the issues with strategies that can be worked on and perfected as the individual progresses and changes. Such conditions as FASD, ASD, PTSD and Neglect and abuse effects are workable, and there are many examples of how they can be improved with good parenting, teaching, professional intervention and self-belief. We will never be able to formulate a solution to everyone's behavioural issues and difficulties, but each small step we improve is a huge progression, and is more likely to build a secure and strengthened base for the individual to add to, and strengthen further, with help, reminders and strategies. We must appreciate that a secure and stable base is essential to the success and progression.

We identify each of the behaviours and discuss the likely successful strategies with simple workable ideas in the next area of the book, and look forward to taking you on a journey of exploration of behaviours, difficulties and 'real life' examples of what has worked in practice.

Chapter 3
Us – Carers, Professionals, Parents, Etc.

Who can say they have learned everything? I think we all agree that no one, apart from the closed minded, stupid and bigoted, can say that. We are ever evolving, learn something new every day, and even more importantly, we continue to learn about ourselves each and every day – if we allow ourselves to. I know I have uncovered and discovered many skills I never realised I had in the past few years, and I continually amaze myself how much information I already knew, but did not know where to find it – as I never needed to use it.

As humans, as parents, as professionals etc. we have banked an enormous amount of knowledge in our brain, and it is up to us to explore the 'toolbox' we already possess to find strategies, skills, knowledge and experiences that will help us to deal with differing situations in all areas of life, but specifically in working with a younger person as the more we can relate to that person, the more they will respond and believe/trust. You will shock yourselves as to the skills you have built up and have not used, once you begin to open your mind to exploring other avenues and strategies to help a young person, with the simple techniques and strategies that we discuss in this book.

It is also very important that we continue to learn, and I would urge anyone involved with children displaying the difficulties and behaviours in this book to attend as many parenting groups, support groups (condition specific or otherwise) and educational forums as they possibly can. There are an amazing amount of free online University short courses available and there are some very reasonably priced distance learning courses that you will be able to access. There are many examples throughout the text in this book and please refer to the glossary at the rear of the book to find out more.

Do not get involved in the 'coffee morning' style groups or feel the need to share stories with others 'Jeremy Kyle' style as these are very often negative forms of communication and do not aim to resolve or build strategies. We are interested in forming positive outcomes and progressive techniques, not topping another anecdote with a more shocking or extreme one. Never become involved in negative discussions about professional bodies or authorities that are there to help us, as believe it or not, they are there to help us, and you will find if you are communicative in the correct manner, that nine times out of ten you will be successful in gaining the help you require. I have lots of experience in this area, and have managed to gain lots of help and support, where others have failed, achieving some huge positives e.g. gaining access to University for a young lady with FASD who could not master maths, and the University were happy to waive the necessity for GCSE maths, based on that young lady's personal statement, tutor's comments and results in other academic areas. If you always put yourself in another's shoes and appreciate what constraints they are working under, you will make more sense of the situation, the barriers that need to be overcome, and you will process a positive and persuasive outcome, advocating for the young person in the most efficient manner. Be patient, sensitive focused and assertive.

Never turn down any training that is offered to you, even if it seems unnecessary at the time. You will learn something, and on many occasions, the training will serve to reaffirm the positive actions and strategies that you already employ. Training and learning is very much about people, and people continue to learn, progress and experience many different things, thus we can always learn from them and their experiences, whilst an experience of ours may spark another line of thinking within the group and build a whole new potential strategy that could be the answer to a conundrum that has been puzzling us. As previously mentioned, 'we build a bank of knowledge' and although today's training may not be useful today, it may well be valuable in future weeks, months or years. I am constantly frustrated by people saying 'I don't need to attend that session – I am not looking after/working with/needing to understand anyone with that issue' or even worse 'oh we have done that one before – what's the point?'. The greatest training I have experienced have been the sessions where we have revisited areas we have previously discussed and have gained a greater perspective over time, allowing us to make mistakes, test, try and perfect the techniques and strategies ensuring a positive outcome for all.

People change, situations change, people progress, people grow – we must never believe we can provide all that we need to the young people we work with, if we do not continue to learn, grow, progress, keep up with the current trends, understand the current pressures, social networks etc.

Preparation is very important too. Have a set of questions you wish to answer before engaging with any client, young person, professional, training session, support group etc. You may not answer them immediately, but they will be considered, tabled and ready to be discussed further at later opportunities. Follow up if necessary via email, and do not get frustrated if you cannot find the answer and do not be afraid to ask the same question again, based upon the evidence of the paragraph above.

We also discuss, towards the end of this book, the undeniable need for 'Us' to look after ourselves. This is of paramount importance, and we must, if we wish to succeed, be consistent, relaxed, feel strong in mind and be physically fit. Respite and clever scheduling of our lives is required to keep us on 'top of our game', and we must always be aware that often, we are working on behalf of two or more brains and this is mentally exhausting. Protect yourself, look after yourself, make time for yourself and feel good about yourself

– and of course, read to the end of this book to help yourself, then keep it close at hand 'in the glovebox' in case you need to refer to it when something does not feel as if it is running as smoothly as we would like.

Chapter 4
Distractions

Very often, children with behavioural difficulties will have extreme issues with getting distracted all too easily, causing them to lose focus and concentration leading to diminished learning, frustration, and in many cases, anger, rudeness or tantrums. In some cases, such as children on the Autistic spectrum, this will not be the case as they can be extremely focused, and sometimes quite the opposite in terms of not being able to pull them away from their particular task or activity, especially if it is their specialised subject and place of safety.

Each child needs careful consideration when assessing and identifying their needs surrounding the removal and cleansing of distractions as some will find safety, and a feeling of comfort with some of the items that you may feel are distracting them, and what is considered 'the norm' is often the opposite i.e. a child placed with us feels severe comfort in chewing gum at all times when asked to concentrate, behave, be quiet, listen and learn, but this most definitely goes against what we would consider good parenting and good manners, especially in the classroom setting. This situation needs to be carefully weighed up, as it is not necessarily breaking the rules to give in to a child, but could also be seen as a carefully chosen tool to not only the aide the learning of the child in question, but also the others around her.

School is a particularly difficult one, as all classrooms are full of clutter and useful information, plus stimulation of the brain promotes learning in most cases. In some cases, it would be preferential for the child who is easily distracted to learn in a plain and clear environment to help them to focus on one single task. We can trial this at home in the children's bedrooms and you will find that each child responds differently to each different environment. It is best to subtly and slowly remove clutter, if you currently feel this may be an issue that could help the child to sleep, focus on homework, help them play etc. and also consider the materials that are present in the room – see Chapter 36 for more information and strategies. We have experienced one child who is now an adult, who believed that she liked a 'busy' bedroom with lots of posters, colours, soft furnishings as 'that is what girls do and like', but when we gradually removed the contents and the distractions, she became much calmer, much better at sleeping, much more focused on self-care and hygiene, showed a huge improvement in her ability to be organised, and have all the tools she needed for school or college along with her recognition that she felt 'less closed in and smothered with stuff', so much so that when we visit her at her Halls of Residence at University, we see a 'cell' type room that she has created for herself with a simple bed, plain cover, everything in drawers or hanging in a closed wardrobe, and a clear desk and empty cork wall board. There is one list on the desk that is a timetable of daily tasks and a box with all of the photos that students would usually keep on the wall, but she is unable to sleep and focus on work studies with 'all that lot gawping at me!'.

With much smaller children, it is sensible to minimise the items that could distract them – not only in their bedroom, but also in the common areas of the house. Good closed storage solutions often help and adult supervision when removing toys, pens, books from any cupboard is advised to focus the child on what they really want and are going to occupy themselves with. Decisions are often very difficult and frustrating processes for our children, and the narrower these become the easier it is for them to succeed in the task that they want or need to focus on. We can help.

Chapter 5
Problem Solving and
Mathematical Issues

For many reasons, children process information in different ways, and this can affect their ability to make sense of instructions, patterns, numbers, letters, and their overall skill to picture and process. We all sit somewhere on the Autistic Spectrum and therefore, it is important that we understand that everyone processes differently in terms of speed, sense, emotion, capability, coping mechanisms and even more simple processes of the brain, such as colour, smell and taste. We must promote as much imaginative thinking as possible and allow each individual child to express their emotions, artistic flair and imagination, also being mindful that they may not possess the ability to process these elements. Time and Money will often prove very difficult for some, and as we believe they are 'obvious', we can become frustrated with the inability of someone to grasp these concepts, and the most intelligent of person can sometimes struggle to apply both as they are 'concepts' and are not obvious to all brain patterns, especially ones affected by Trauma, Attachment, Neglect and in almost all cases of Foetal Alcohol Spectrum Disorder.

'Don't know' will be a very regular participant in many of your conversations with children that are displaying as being 'difficult', but embrace the fact that this is an acceptable phrase that is genuine and should always be welcomed with the retort 'I know you don't know, so let's try and make sense of it together', whilst attempting to approach the conundrum from another direction, perhaps, with fewer words or simpler language. Never assume that someone who is unable to freely process or problem solve is being lazy, difficult, oppositional or just plain awkward, as very often your inability to understand that they cannot, causes increased friction, shame, more opposition, rudeness and anger, resulting in a complete inability to accept your teaching. This will take skill and knowledge, and will be ever changing – sorry to break the bad news, but when you feel you have 'made a breakthrough', this will often be a temporary success, and may not apply to all instances and the next interaction with this individual. Be patient.

A young person in my care for over 9 years who is now in her early 20's finds it enormously difficult to process the finer elements of time and money. She completed a degree course at University (having been accepted with a functional Maths certificate as long as she accepted help from the disability team) and she copes by using the strategy of hours and full pounds only. Minutes and pence cause huge issues in her processing ability and phase her enough to make her fail at being able to spend and save or be on time. By ignoring the minor elements, she can cope with life and will always use the strategy of being the hour earlier, i.e. if her engagement is 9.30am, she will arrive for 9am and cope with being early. In a similar form, we built the strategy that if she concentrates on ensuring she has the correct change or payment to the next pound, she will always be covered and at worst, be 99p worse off. She has built on this strategy over the years and can cope with smaller amounts of change if involved with smaller amounts initially, but minutes are still a step too far.

I am still, six years on teaching an 11 year old to cross the road safely as each new road brings its own new patterns and problems. We can even revert back to the same road with different cars and times of the day to highlight a whole new set of problems. This young person is just below average at mainstream Primary School (but has a reading age of one whole year above her age) and can problem solve many areas, but does have severe memory and processing issues that seem to affect this very important area of everyday life. We will succeed.

Chapter 6
We Can Help

How can we help to achieve results?

First of all, we can change how we address the issues and the person, ensuring we are clear and simple in our language, instructing the young person of what they must do. Never tell them what not to do, as this is a very confusing concept. Negative comments, raised voices and impatience in the Teacher/Adult result in negative, loud and angry responses from the young person causing failure, and a breakdown in communication.

Always attempt to ask yourself how the young person would best understand the instruction you wish to give and do not be afraid to use too few words. To explain, some brains process very simply, some logically, others literally, and some are only able to hear and make sense of very few, possibly only single words. If you want a child to take a seat, say 'Please sit down' and see what happens. I have known a child sit on the floor, ignoring chairs around them and have also experienced one who sat on the table. One extreme young man, of whom I was helping his adoptive parents since almost birth, cope with his now 'more difficult' behaviours at age 9, decided he would take a seat on top of a bookcase in the library area of the Primary School we were meeting in, so I smiled at him, and said, 'Shall I come up there too?' and he politely said, 'No, you are quite fat and it will probably fall to pieces'. He was possibly correct and then decided himself that to talk he would be better coming down, as we carried on without him and he could not hear what we were saying.

Sometimes, it is best to start at the simplest point and assume that the young person needs as much help as is possible to make sense of an instruction, and this can feel like you are addressing a pet or an elderly person
that is either hard of hearing or suffering from Dementia, but said in the correct tone, it will be non-threatening and is in my experience, very relieving for the young person who is heightened, nervous, feeling awkward or just plain distracted. You can always work up from there as you get to know the person and their capabilities, but always be mindful not to become complacent, and use too many words, expecting that they will be able to process efficiently.

We can restrict choices to help them too. When processing is difficult, making decisions is an enormous pressure, especially when it comes to important ones such as food, drink, toilet and what to do next. We find list and menus are an enormous relief to many young people who find consistent behaviours, and processing difficult to maintain and cope with. Do not be afraid to reduce choices, believing you are being too controlling or not allowing them to express themselves, if you genuinely perceive that decision making causes anxiety and many 'don't knows'. When I first knew one young lady, she always wanted the same choices as everyone else in our foster family as she felt otherwise this was not fair. This would always end up in her choosing an item that she did not like (quite often desserts). She has memory and processing issues, thus the strategy of giving her a long list of options, naming the one we knew she liked at the very end of the list, ensured she picked that one and was always happy. As she has progressed, we explained to her that this was the strategy and that it was invented to help her make a good choice, but that now she must make her own good choices based upon the fact that she knows what she likes, and if necessary (as we did), keep a list of the desserts that she prefers to ensure she always picks one from the list. She will still attempt to go 'off the chosen path' at times of tiredness or when she is feeling 'low' and we have allowed her to, knowing the outcome (spitting it out), but then reminding her why the list is in place.

Finally and most importantly, take a moment to reflect and remind yourself that we can help by being calm, patient, understanding, clear, concise, positive, and always ask yourself, 'can I help this young person make sense of this issue at this moment when they are in this position?' the answer will always be in the negative, thus we must allow thought, reflection and sometimes, the mood or event to simply 'blowout' or 'blow-over'. We must always allow ourselves time and space to make sense of what has happened, and if we believe the young person can make sense of it, that we can advise, discuss and resolve. If we are not sure or know the young person is incapable of making sense of the incorrect behaviour or habitual problem, it is best to wait and use many of the other strategies that we will discuss throughout this book.

Chapter 7
They Can Listen

As you will all be very aware of and quite possibly frustrated with, all children can listen when they want to – or more to the point, when there is something in it for them. This does not mean we have to reward physically, but it does mean we have to be clever in our approaches, and with what and how we use our words and instructions, persuading the often vulnerable young person that there is something in this for them, thus it is worth listening.

In some cases with very basic children – no matter what age – we can use the simple and very direct language 'ssshhh – close your mouth and think/or use your brain' or 'wait, take a quiet moment to process what I said and then tell me' depending on how you have chosen to address the children you are working with leave them for between 15 and 45 seconds before repeating the question or asking them if they remember the question or instruction prior to continuing. I use all three with different children that I look after and work with regularly, and they appreciate the very clear instruction and the fact that I have reminded them how best to process their thoughts before committing to an answer, ensuring they have understood and have the best chance of making a sensible answer, decision or statement.

If the situation is slightly less calm and/or potentially dangerous or violent, never be afraid to raise your voice and say very clearly 'stop'. Stop is a very clear instruction and does not need any further words added to it – most humans will stop immediately if requested in a confident, stern tone of voice and if the young person is visible, also use a full flat hand in front of your face towards them signalling the same. Once calmer, return to the steps above, and ensure they have listened and understood, clearly advising them that you will discuss the issue when they have calmed, and you are sure they can understand what needs to be communicated.

Some children will love negative attention, but if you are silent and patient they will, in most cases, climb down from their unacceptable behaviour and want to hear what you have to say. Do not turn your back on them and always maintain your eyes being directed at them at all times – not directly at their eyes, as they may see this as confrontational. If they use phrases like 'what are you looking at?', the simple and calm reply of 'I am ensuring you are safe and am waiting for you to be calm'. Never tell them they look stupid, childish or immature during this event, whilst they are heightened and acting out, but do explain to them when they are calm that you are surprised that they behaved like this as you know they can be more mature, want to be more mature and want to be treated as a more mature young person.

Chapter 8
The Same Mistake

The young people we are discussing in this book, will inevitably make the same mistake many times and for many different reasons, whether that be through pre-birth damage to their brain, early life damage, neglect, a lack of care of other significant reason, we can always help them to alleviate this by making it acceptable but very much a topic of conversation and learning – not criticism or ridicule. A very effective strategy for opening up discussion and thought on this subject – which will be very sensitive as no one likes to be wrong, look stupid or be told they have made the same mistake again – is to verbally express 'oops silly me I made a mistake' and if necessary make mistakes intentionally to exaggerate the necessity to bring discussion into play. All young people love to know and see that adults make mistakes.

As adults, we can help the young person make mistakes and accept them by setting them tasks where we know they will fail, but we can support them and hopefully, discuss how we can work on this to see if we can make more sense of the issue next time. We must go at a pace they can cope with and we must never
accelerate learning to move onto the next step until we are sure they have grasped this one – be happy to cross the same road tens of times, before attempting the next one, and show the young person what happens, by making a safe mistake yourself i.e. go to cross and say 'is this safe to cross now?' very loudly. They will advise you, and you will gauge where their learning and understanding is at. Swimming is a great test if you are confident in the water, as you can allow them

to make a mistake and save them. We do these things naturally with very young children over their early years and it becomes second nature, but we must never take these things for granted or leave these very simple stones unturned in older children/young adults who have entered our care somewhat later, as they are the important building blocks to making good decisions. It is obviously very important also to ensure these young people are being tested and allowed to make mistakes in a safe environment as it is our role to make them as independent as possible as early as we can.

Rewards for progression on making the same mistake should be topic appropriate and well thought out, so that they make complete sense, and can be linked to the area of concern. This ultimately means that trust and the extending of boundaries will very often be the reward. This can be difficult, but do not be fearful and manage the situation in such a way that progression is stunted or not recognised. Never dangle the rewards prior to the achievement as they may become frustrating and/or bored by them – the element of surprise is always a much more exciting feeling than achieving something you expected, thus will naturally ensure the young person will wish to strive to achieve next time.

Never be afraid to make mistakes yourself within this process as you can never lose, always using 'oh silly me I made a mistake' and adding 'I am going to learn from that one'.

Chapter 9
Developmental Appropriate Play – Fill the Gaps

As I am sure many of you are already recognising, young people with behavioural issues act much younger than their chronological age in many ways, if not all. One of the areas that is very difficult to understand is the subject of play. Ask yourself these questions:-

- How do we play?
- What is play?
- Who should play with who?
- Is it ok to play alone?
- Is it better to play in groups or one to one?
- What do kids like to play?
- Can they play?
- Do they like to play?

Play means many different things to many people and is not universally understood or enjoyed by all. It is a very conceptual process that requires lots of different parts of the brain to be functioning in tandem correctly and is a lot more difficult than most believe.

The most important thing with regard to play is that it is fun for the participant/s. There will be many different factors and ideas, with some young people choosing quite simply not to engage in play as they do not understand the rules and boundaries that are regularly associated with it. If we break it down, it is enormously complex, and requires understanding and ability in language, coordination, gross and fine motor skills, processing, and multi-tasking, all whilst trying to have fun.

Start at the basics for everyone who comes into your care and never assume. We were lucky enough to be able to teach a 15 year old young lady to master the skill of catching and throwing a ball to a partner only 3 ft. away. Her early life pattern had been so chaotic, that this was really not high on the list of skills that were required to maintain a safe and healthy existence. There were lots of tears, embarrassment, and moments of feeling useless and awkward, but with lots of patience, understanding and some amazing other children, we supported this young lady to achieve something she deemed impossible, and far too late to grasp. She will now be able to play catch with her own children one day and this is priceless.

There are no rights and wrongs with regard to play and its correctness or necessity, but it does involve interaction, care, and often togetherness. This is a major positive in working with any young person, and can build trust, emotions, feelings, imagination, thought processing and skills that can be transferred to many other areas of life – without too many words and making this obvious that we are undertaking this much larger, more intense task.

Try all of the different forms of play, and if possible, attempt to fill the gaps (at whatever age) to assess where the young person feels most comfortable and how it is best to allow them to express themselves through play.

You will sometimes come across children who cannot play. Do not worry and do not force it. It does not always requires toys, other people or a particular pattern at a certain age. Be inventive, be imaginative and start at simple – I-spy is play, walking the dog is play, washing up is play and clapping your hands is play. There is no particular pattern and progression that we have to mirror or prove, but always assess each event that you consider play, so that you can make future decisions based on what the young person enjoys and feels comfortable in performing.

This is a huge subject and has so many factors that we can only scratch the surface in this publication. There are many specific publications and programmes identifying play, but many of them will crossover and often contradict each other, and I have many examples of where professional 'play therapy' has been very useful and productive, but equally many that have felt it had no impact at all and was a waste of time. This to me proves it is a very personal journey for all young people and needs to be investigated over time in natural surroundings, thus we are the most appropriately qualified people to undertake and mange this important element.

Chapter 10
Transitions

A transition is quite simply any change that takes place in our lives.

I have looked after children that find huge difficulty in the daily transitions of waking, eating breakfast, going to and from school, eating meals, getting in and out of a car, and going to bed – these are mostly owing to ASD, FASD, Trauma and neglect. I have equally looked after other children that find these 'minor' transitions very simple, but cannot cope with unstructured times such as break times, lunchtimes, holidays and school trips. I refer to these as medium strength transitions and these are often made difficult by a lack of self-esteem, confidence, low school attendance or issues within social settings. Then, of course, there are

the much larger transitions which make most people anxious and include changing schools, moving home, going into hospital, becoming an adult etc. – we all deal with these in our own way, but we mostly cope and make sense of them as we have always had support and safety in our families, and have been supported, counselled and have witnessed others making these alterations to their lives without issue or danger, thus allowing us to overcome our fears.

Children in more difficult situations or with different brain patterns will have many strategies for coping with these areas of life – often they will seem obscure and nonsensical. We can alleviate the fears associated with these events with careful consideration and associated strategies. An example of this would be to make a presentation to a child on the proposed holiday destination which includes photographs of where it is, how their room will look, what food looks and tastes like, asking them what they feel could be an issue for them so that you can overcome this as a team.

Another example of this would be to display the menu of the food you are going to serve on which day in your home so that the child can predict and feel comfortable knowing that they will be fed, and what they can expect – knowing they like it.

Purposely, make transitions happen for this person in the areas that they feel less comfortable in – i.e. Send them on a small one night break/respite to another family home ensuring you drop them off and collect them exactly at the time you said you would, allowing them to trust that what they knew would happen, did happen. This can then be built up and extended, ensuring they can enjoy such events as school residential trips and adventure groups. Make very simple changes within your home environment and explain why you are doing it – i.e. Change the seat they sit at the table or in the car regularly, enabling them to see that change can be safe and can be sometimes better, worse or possibly the preferred outcome 'nothing changes really'. The skill of extending boundaries, and assessing their ability to cope and feel comfortable with transition can only be gauged with trial and error in real examples and situations, but if we consider the following points, we will always make good decisions and healthy progression:-

- The timing of the transition – always at a calm and uneventful period
- Feelings – always consider their thoughts and ask them how they feel
- Confidence – show you are confident in the event/process and voice this
- Communication – tell them why you are trialling this
- Facts – be precise and tenacious allowing them to know what is happening
- Show and tell – make sure they can see, taste and smell what's in store for them

- Surprise – can achieve huge progress, but needs careful knowledge and skill by you

You will experience many different scenarios, but as long as you bear the elements listed above in mind on all occasions, you will be prepared and will progress. Always de-brief, and recall the event with the young person, appraising the positive and negative feelings and thoughts, asking them how they feel this could be improved, make them feel safer, more comfortable etc.

Never be afraid to test their ability to extend their boundaries and resilience, but always be mindful of the 'pieces' you may have to pick up post event. You will also notice, if given any amount of time with the same young person, that things will progress and quite possibly regress. This is due to a feeling of comfort in being supported and nurtured by someone who we trust, which is preferable to many than trusting/relying on their own instincts, abilities or organisation. It is our job to give the young person the best grounding and advice that we can during our time with them, ultimately, ensuring they become a functioning adult that can enjoy the fruits of independence and the safe exploration of the world around us. Sometimes, you will need to 'cram' these elements into a much shorter span than a complete childhood, but attempt as many as you can, as even if they do not make full sense of it in the moment, it may remain in their memory bank and reappear when required in later life.

Chapter 11
Simple Instructions

One of the most imperative skills we must maintain, and keep at the forefront of our minds when working with and helping a young person who shows the distractive, disorganised and non-compliant traits we regularly witness, is the ability to address the child directly and efficiently with simple concise, and easily understood instructions. We all use slang, code and obscure references in everyday speak that are conceptual, and make no sense to the black and white brain patterns of the child with difficulties in processing. Here are some nonsensical examples:-

- Pull your socks up/buck your ideas up
- Get dressed
- Tidy up that mess
- Hurry up/you've got 5 minutes until we go out the door
- Sleep tight

We all use these, and most of you will feel they are possibly clear and that it is even obvious what they mean – this is because you have been conditioned over many years and can see the concept form a reality. To the child with an autistic trait and obscure processing, these mean nothing, and need breaking down into simple language that is measurable (don't forget they do not understand time) and achievable to the particular child you are addressing and instructing. Initially, it will seem odd, but I can guarantee it will make your life easier if you use more specific instructions.

It is important to also address the young person by first using their name prior to asking them to follow any instruction as until you have engaged their specific brain and attention, they will not recognise or react to your instruction quickly enough. This is particularly important if you are addressing a group and you may have to engage several children/pupils/siblings. Take your time and practice with some of the following simple clear instructions, and adapt them as necessary for the areas that your young person / people:-

- Jane… you need to improve your behaviour. Look at me and listen please.
- John… put your trousers on. Put your shirt on. Now put these shoes on…
- Kevin… look at all those books on the floor. Put them back onto this shelf please.
- Lee… we need to be quick. Have you got your pencil case? Have you got your lunch?
- Sophie… get in bed. Pull your cover over you. Put your head on the pillow and sleep nicely.

You will very quickly notice how efficient this strategy makes the children and young people you are working with, and how it removes many of the battles you may have experienced and believed were 'oppositional' behaviours. You will also very likely notice how relieved the young person seems and how they can perform a task as you would expect. Again, it is our pattern of thinking that needs to change to suit their pattern of thinking, quite simply as ours can change and theirs cannot. If ever you find yourself becoming frustrated and saying 'it's obvious' or 'oh my god can it really be that difficult' – re-evaluate your instruction, and try a different angle of approach to ensure you are clear and are simplifying the instruction for the other person. I cannot give you the perfect answer to all of the patterns of your subjects individual brains and do not know what capacity they have to understand 'conceptual' instructions or slang/local dialect, but you will form this in time, with practice and patience. If you do find yourself not being clear enough, use this opportunity to apologise to the young person/s, and vocalise the fact that you are going to attempt to make it simple and help them to understand, asking them to wait whilst you think of an improved instruction – humour will often come into play and this can only be a positive so feel free to make mistakes, and use the earlier strategies we discussed.

Chapter 12
Sleep

The 'norm' as far as sleep goes is a complete fantasy. There is no such thing and never will be. Many societies across the world utilise very different sleep patterns and strategies, and in many instances, the supposed 'norm' causes a huge amount of stress and confrontation, which can easily be avoided if you remove the current thought pattern you very rigidly believe. This is quite possibly the 'perfect 8 hours sleep for adults and 10 hours for children'. The brain patterns, and learned behaviours of young people affected by the issues we are discussing and working with ensure that they will present very obscure sleep patterns.

FASD affected children, for example, can be complete opposite ends of the sleep spectrum, some needing 12 hours sleep and some quite literally not sleeping at all. There is no hard and fast rule as to what is a healthy sleep, and each individual will require observation, new strategies, different surroundings and very different help to ensure they are getting enough sleep or rest allowing them to function at their most efficient.

Remove the rules and the 'norm', and work with all of the skills and strategies you know about sleep in the different age groups, cultures, and individuals that you know or have read about.

Many extremely successful world leaders, and successful business men and women boast of very irregular sleep patterns – some sleeping for only 2-4 hours per night and some having afternoon naps, along with the possible enhancement of meditation, needing music to be playing, and usually some quite odd routines around going to bed/sleep.

We have found that strategies such as removing the stimulation of the brain via the use of screens much earlier than sleep time, helps the brain to calm and relax in many of the children we have looked after – at least, one hour before bed time, and possible reading or listening to music helps them to relax and form a healthier sleep pattern. For the children that only require a few hours' sleep, the introduction of headphones and the understanding that they must be quiet for the other people in the house often allows them to formulate healthier rest periods for all. A good old fashioned soft toy works wonders, and should always be allowed and never mocked. One young man who would like to think he was a 'bit of a gangster' slept with his favourite Husky soft toy through until he was 17 years old and this helped him to calm as he regularly talked through his day with his 'dog', and made sense of the world and his worries.

Some physical strategies that can be implemented can be bathing or showering before bed if this relaxes the young person, whilst the use of weighted blankets, and 'over bed tents' can also help to keep the young person feeling safe and cocooned from distraction, and very often, their irregular thoughts and fears. One young lad who we looked after could not cope with a bedroom much bigger than his bed, thus we allowed him to swap bedrooms with his younger sister allowing him to feel safer. When we moved him up to a larger bedroom, we increased the size of the bed and this made him feel safer also.

Another myth around sleep is comfort. Do not assume that what you believe is comfortable is to another. We once allowed an 11 year old lad to sleep fully dressed for six whole months as he felt safer and more relaxed if he maintained the comfort of his clothes. We celebrated when he, eventually, came down in the pyjamas we had left in his drawer as we knew that he was feeling safer and wanted to parade this. It was a very simple way of him expressing his feelings without saying the words or giving away too much control, and he will still recall this today and laugh about it now he is in his early twenties. If we would have insisted he 'gets dressed for bed', he would have felt extremely vulnerable and out of control, possibly delaying his progression and feelings of safety/comfort in his surroundings. He would sometimes express his imbalance by sleeping upside down or on the floor, and to allow him to do this helped him to make sense of his feelings, emotions and measure how he was progressing. This pattern did form again when he left the family home and entered independence age 19, but he was aware of it and could voice why he was feeling this way, making sense of it, ultimately, allowing him to build strategies to overcome this areas of his life that caused the imbalance within his mind.

Never be afraid to try differing strategies as you cannot really 'ruin' a sleep pattern that is not an efficient and healthy one, and it is important that you give the options and keep an open mind as to what could be the ideal solution. This does not mean it will always be the perfect solution, thus be aware of the continuing issues that subjects such as sleep will bring to young people with differing brain patterns and capabilities, when many of the other areas of the chapters in this book come into play i.e. Transitions, social difficulties, emotions, puberty etc.

Chapter 13
Pain

This does not mean 'they are a pain!' ha ha.

Pain is a very interesting part of the human brain and its processing capabilities. Many of the young people you will work with will have very obscure pain thresholds, whether that be very weak, very strong or extremely obscure and sometime nonsensical. A young lady who we looked after for several years was extremely complex in many ways and her sense of pain was unbelievably obscure. She would 'jump out of her skin' and scream profusely if a fly landed on her arm or leg – she was not scared of or 'freaked out' by flies – ending up shaking, and experiencing large floods of adrenalin, whereas we saw her experience much greater pain in the form of falls, being knocked flying into the air by our 75kg Great Dane, along with sporting injuries that wounded her, only to see her laugh them off and not even realise that pain was present until many minutes, sometimes, hours later?. This also extended to her ability to make sense of her body's external temperature in extreme hot or cold and she would regularly walk out into a bitter winter day in tiny inappropriate items of clothing, not realising she felt cold until she literally turned blue. There was no explanation for the reason behind this, but it is recognised that children diagnosed with neglect, trauma, FASD, and sometimes, autistic elements do display such oddities in their patterns of feeling and experiencing pain.

It is important that we allow the young person to experience these elements and feelings, and help them to make sense of them, even if it is only describing how we feel, and what our bodies are experiencing and where. On a cold day walk out before the child in a flimsy item of clothing that is obviously unsuitable and voice 'wow I did not know it was this cold today – I am going to put a thicker coat on' or something to that effect.

Equally allow them to safely experience pain in as many areas of their body areas as possible i.e. A scientific experiment that you record and report which allows them to undertake such actions as pricking their finger with a pin, pulling the hairs on their arm, pinching their ear etc., whilst you, or someone else does the same, and voices the feeling and effect it has on your body and brain/pain threshold.

Sometimes, you may find that a young person with obscure or what you feel may be irregular pain issues finds comfort in a particular amount of pain. A very young girl who we looked after found it soothing if she gripped her wrist very tightly when she felt scared or imbalanced. It is a complex area of the brain, and can be sometimes extreme and unsafe, but by investigating and experimenting, you will be able to gauge if the young person finds excessive comfort in pain which could lead to areas of self-harm. If this is ever a concern, contact your known professional that can advise and guide you to safe intervention and practice. Never ignore the comfort of pain as it can escalate very quickly and can become extremely dangerous. It is not always our job to directly aide and repair areas of difficulty and concern, thus we must recognise, and safely advise others more capable and professionally engaged in dealing with more complex issues. Our role sometimes needs to be of an advocate and advisor, passing the baton to others who are better placed to work more closely with an issue, and advise either the young person or us how to combat, and strategise safely and efficiently.

Chapter 14
Danger

This bring us nicely into the 'Danger Zone', where it very often can only be our role to recognise more dangerous areas of behaviour and best use our network of professionals in the best interest of our young people. Never be afraid to ask for help – it can never be too early.

Danger is a huge area of concern for all of the children we work with and describe in the category of 'difficult'. Decision making and understanding of situations/consequences is an extremely difficult skill for any young person to master and make sense of, especially when brain function is incomplete, damaged, obscure or irregular, and life experiences have thrown many unusual teachings/learned behaviours their way.

In what areas does your young person actually recognise danger? I would suggest listing the following areas and assessing their conceived ability to make sense of this danger in terms of 'makes sense', 'does not make sense' or 'confused and irregular' when they fluctuate between their understanding and reading of this particular area of danger. You could also break it down into 'safe', 'Dangerous' and/or 'extremely dangerous' if you feel this helps you to see, and realise their abilities and strengths, weaknesses in this area.

Dangers range from the very simple low risk elements to very risky and life threatening extremes, and we must fully understand where and how each one is important to the young people we are working with, and to what extent we must teach them how to strategise for this or protect them if this is the only way we can see to keep them safe. We must, however, not be risk averse and be overprotective as this will only exacerbate the areas of concern at a later stage.

If necessary, use role play intervention, and real life examples to gauge the young person's understanding and recognition of the danger. We have found that the use of Television or Movie examples can work in understanding the areas where they could find difficulty, then progressing these areas on for further development, teaching and understanding in a prioritised form of working to alleviate the risk, and enhance safety. Always, as previously mentioned and advised, highlight to the young person why you are discussing these areas and ensure you use the words 'to keep you safe from being hurt, injured or very ill', **not** to keep you from danger, as again this is a concept that will very likely be a confused one.

- Trip hazards
- Staircases
- Sharp objects in everyday use
- Liquids – chemical cleaners, soaps, hot and cold etc.
- Ability to gauge height and the consequence of a fall
- Ability to gauge depth and the safety around water
- Taste – do they gauge taste and acidity correctly – salt, chillies, lemons test
- Poison – what is safe/unsafe
- Matches and lighters
- Roads and speed awareness
- Playground apparatus
- Trees, walls and climbing
- People
- Violence and weapons
- Sexual dangers and consequences of intercourse – pregnancy and infection
- Predators, grooming etc.
- Alcohol
- Drugs
- Cycling and speed awareness/braking

- Electrical sockets and appliances
- Appropriate dress and privacy around nudity
- Darkness
- Safety around animals
- Stealing and others property
- Sun – burn and the importance of hydration
- Correctly cooked food
- Pans, kettles, irons and ovens
- Online and internet dangers

These are the most common areas of concern and risk to young people, and some will apply at differing ages and levels of ability, but please assess all and make an appraisal of all at regular intervals, involving other professionals and adults who have regular contact with the young people to ensure alternative opinions and vision is considered. Never assume they are not at risk if they have not yet made a mistake in all of these areas and open your mind to put yourself in their shoes as best you can to predict how you feel they would cope if faced with this danger.

As previously mentioned, and definitely worth another mention is DO NOT BE RISK AVERSE and do not protect the child too much. It is our duty to ensure they are best advised, taught and prepared for the correct way of dealing with any risky situation always telling them clearly how to perform the positive action to avoid danger, in preference to 'what not to do'.

Some of the areas will be obvious to the young person and some may surprise you in being completely inept at recognising even the simplest danger, sometimes when they recognise and can strategise to avoid greater dangers.

Going back to my example of earlier in the book, the young lady who 6 years on cannot still safely cross the road at age 11 – if we assumed she was safe once we taught her to cross one road, this would have been a huge mistake, as each road is a very different prospect and vision in the eyes of this young lady, thus we have to practice each individual road we know she is going to have to cross, and make a very simple set of rules that do not allow options; only a fixed route at safe crossing places with no exceptions or time limits. She is fully aware of other dangers such as height risk and falling, climbing and darkness, but cannot make sense of the dangers of people, depth of water, anything to do with fire or online/the dangers of the internet. We have to take each element as a very separate entity and work with each one at the most appropriate point in time. This can also be exaggerated as it is in this case, by an extremely poor working memory, ensuring we need to remind, re-teach and re-enact each area of danger many, many times over.

Chapter 15
Food Control

It is very likely that you will, as an adult working with difficult children, experience many differing patterns of controlling and misunderstanding the worth, necessity and simple nature of food, and what it means. There is always a danger that the more extreme trauma, confused state and/or instances of abuse or neglect will cause very obscure control, around food, when it is eaten, what is eaten and how it is eaten. This can be exacerbated by early life experiences of adopted or looked after children and of course, children who have been affected by alcohol in the womb (FASD).

It is a very delicate area that requires careful strategic planning and implementation. At its minimum, it will cause diet to be very poor and unhealthy, possibly leading to battles and emotional conflict as it becomes harder to alter the habits and control of the young person. At its worst, of course, it can lead to eating disorders, such as Anorexia, Bulimia and complex issues that require professional intervention.

In my experience, it is best to allow any unusual traits around food to play out over time, and report and record them to the necessary professionals, and liaise with any other adults that are working closely with the young person. A good example of this that I can recall clearly is one of an 8 year old fostered young lady, who had been sexually abused at age 5, whilst being heavily neglected and possibly suffering minor malnutrition in the years following as an 'apology' from her birth mother. At placement commencement, it was very obvious that the young lady could not chew and swallow solid food very well at all, often regurgitating the contents of the small amount of food very soon after it had entered her system. It became apparent that she had only been fed egg mayonnaise from premade containers along with 'ready meal' macaroni cheese and lots of ice cream. Her jaw muscles were not adept at chewing, and her muscles in her neck needed to be trained and built to accept solids. The advice we received from the psychologist was 'any solid food is better than nothing'. We attempted chicken, potatoes and carrots as she expressed her affection towards these foods, reminding herself that she used to eat these when she was little, but she could not find the strength to keep them down. We tried toast at breakfast, along with small sandwich triangles with ham, but again, with no success. One of our boys very innocently offered her a Cherry Bakewell as they 'were exceedingly good' and the young lady took her time, rejected the cherry, but completed and kept down the tasty pie. It took three months of Mr Kipling's finest (and a few supermarket own brand ones for good measure) for breakfast to help her move on to a more varied and solid diet, but with lots of help and consultation along the way. Spaghetti Bolognese is still a favourite, and she does prefer easier to digest foods, but she will, now aged 16, regularly consume chicken, ham, bread, vegetables, pasta, pizza and her favourite homemade Fish Pie.

Food control can be less physical or subliminal and can be very much a way of a young person exercising their control over their world. This is very difficult to deal with in the short term, and my advice is to always allow the behaviour to play out over a period of time, allowing you to keep a food diary of what and when they eat. Always be vigilant in checking their spending habits, bags for wrappers and if they immediately make a beeline for the nearest toilet post meal. Keeping this record and assessing the data retrieved will ensure you are seeing the wider picture, and are making sense of the patterns and realistic consumption of an individual. We have experienced young people that refuse to eat or say they are not eating as a punishment to themselves or another person, possibly you, when secretly they are consuming, often very unhealthy food from another source using the lack of acceptance of food as a controlling area. This can be flushed out by approaching the subject sensitively and calmly, using the strategy 'I would feel extremely hungry, weak and pale if I were not eating – I am guessing you are eating somewhere else as you are looking healthy?' quite often they will appreciate the kind attention, but sometimes they may wish to force a 'battle' with you – either way, this strategy will usually ensure they open up in one way or another.

We have experienced one very extreme young lady who convinced herself that it was a good decision to starve herself to ultimately end her life as she was unhappy, but could not endure any pain that committing suicide in any other, potentially painful, method would bring. Upon consultation with the Psychologist, 3 days in to the behaviour (and upon confirmation that she was definitely not eating or drinking anything), it was felt that a possible strategy could be to advise her graphically how this option would pan out, and that it would cause her lots of stomach pains, headaches, along with almost certain organ damage, ensuring she would be hospitalised and fed via a tube up her nose, whilst nurses prodded and poked her over the many days and even weeks she would remain in hospital. I sat quietly with her and calmly related this scenario to her on the evening of day 4, and very quickly she made the decision to drink a glass of water, soon after agreeing that it was not the best course of action sating 'I am so hungry – can I have my dinner?'. It was not a complete quick fix, obviously and I do not wish to make light of a very complex situation, but it is a very simplified example of using a calculated strategy that reflected on her fear of pain to alleviate the immediate danger, giving us and medical professionals more time to build a full picture of where her issues really lay, helping her to make sense of these areas, and identifying further solutions and strategies to build her strength and self-esteem. This is a work in progress, and I will refer to this young lady in greater depth in up and coming chapters.

Chapter 16
Thank You vs Sorry

A recent strategy that I have introduced is the use of the words 'thank you' as a replacement for the word 'sorry'. There are a few small studies that identify this as a strategy in professional life, marriage, family reparation etc., but I feel it is an amazingly important one in the field of children who find it difficult to maintain healthy and correct/expected behaviours. The main reason I believe this is that it is a positive and healthy reaction that allows further positive dialogue, rather than the almost submissive, negative word 'sorry' that is quite often meaningless, misunderstood, and repetitively boring. 'Thank you' is always positive and welcomes a positive response – you can also play with foreign versions of 'thank you' to alleviate any risk of repetitiveness. This was one of my main motivations, as upon learning Egyptian Arabic, as I have been for the past two years, the word 'Shukran' (pronounced shoe-kran) is Egyptian Arabic for thank you and the word 'afwan' (pronounced with a long vowel af-waan) as the retort 'you're welcome' always makes me smile, thus we introduced this as a replacement for 'sorry', and either 'no you are not', 'say it like you mean it' or 'but I bet you will do it again' being very often the retort of frustrated parents of friends who frequent with children who find it difficult to regulate, remember or maintain their calmness/politeness.

When my 11 year old foster daughter, who has been placed here with our family since she was 4 years old now says 'thank you' when she forgets how to behave, respond or maintain her manners, I am able to say either 'afwan' 'you're welcome', 'no problem' or 'what are you thanking me for?'

with a smile. Her reply will be something like (as we have discussed and agreed) 'thank you for helping me to understand', 'thank you for being patient', thank you for not telling me off', 'thank you for being calm' or something along those lines. In reply to this, I can then progress on to saying 'why would I be impatient when I know your memory has not allowed you to store that information' or 'can you remember how you should have behaved/responded?' It is a strategy I am very confident in and enjoy using very much – I do hope you can manage to introduce it in to your discussions and teachings, as I am sure you will agree and reap the benefits of this very simple change.

Sorry, 'sorry', but you are so last year!

Chapter 17
Emotion, Affection and Not Taking Things Personally

The strategy we just worked through, leads nicely onto the very progressive tool that is NOT taking things personally or allowing emotions and affections cloud the issue. People is an emotional business, and one that regularly results in totally unnecessary battles, conflict, grudges, name calling and tears and tantrums – and that's just the adults !

How do we remove our emotions, I hear you say?

'Very simply' is my reply. Emotions cause misjudgement and confusion. We can all agree and quite possibly recall an instance where have argued with someone we do not know, and have remained unemotional, completely rational and have made a sensible compromised outcome to the issue that required discussion and consultation to resolve. I appreciate you may also be able to recall instances when this has not been the case, but you will definitely agree you feel better about the calmer ones. I do know some people that would still disagree with that and I think I may have been one of them many years ago.

Emotion clouds judgement, and puts barriers in the way of reasoned thinking, especially if you feel wronged and take it personally. I would suggest that we have all felt this way, and have been disappointed by someone else and their actions, possibly to the point of being upset. If you label this behaviour as 'non-personal' and not an attack on you or your personality or authority, it takes on a whole different light and you will be able to reasonably assess the behaviour as you would watching the scenario play out between two other people on

TV, in the street, at school or wherever. Take yourself higher than the scene and attempt to 'look in at it' appraising what is actually being said, done or acted out. Tell yourself:-

- 'This behaviour is nothing to do with me.
- Where is it coming from?
- What could be the reason behind it?
- How many layers down is this behaviour building from?'

When you start to ask yourself these questions, you are successfully removing the personal element of the situation, and you will find very quickly that you find reason and sense in what is being 'played out'. We all know the very infamous 'terrible twos' and we know why they happen – babies and toddlers are exploring the boundaries, and the extent they can push their behaviours too, but we very rarely take this personally, and we often smile knowingly as to 'the rules of engagement' and how this will 'play out'.

A strategy I utilised with a very extreme young lady for the three years between the age of 14 and 17 was to remove the personal element, and to stay very calm, whilst she played out some very abusive language, threats and criticisms of my position. I would wait for the optimum opportunity when she would become heightened and feel she was gaining control, quickly interjecting with a completely nonsensical word such as 'Tuesday'. This interjection would disrupt her flow of abuse and taunting behaviours, and would eventually 'sink in'. When it processed, she would say 'Tuesday what?'. I would purposely pause, stare into space and say 'who said Tuesday?'. Almost immediately, she lost the power that she believed she had and this calmed the situation as I could say 'how can we help you resolve this problem?'. To which she would very often answer something along the lines of 'oh it doesn't matter now' or 'I can't remember what I was saying now'. The word was not consistently 'Tuesday' and could be anything of choice, but it is well worth a try, as it does seem to diffuse a volatile situation that quite often you can see no real answer to or as we said seems like it is a personal attack.

Another strategy I have used, but very carefully, is to mirror the unacceptable behaviour of the child forcing them to raise the question 'what are you doing?' or 'are you crazy or something?'. My favourite one of these was in a very large toyshop mid child tantrum 'I want, I want, bla, bla, bla' with lots of screaming stamping and trashing of aisles etc. I could not reason with my young 7 year old lady, and so I joined the 'party' and screamed at the top of my voice 'aaaarrggghhhh' in a very childish manner. She stopped immediately and looked horrified that I would make this play. She looked at me and wanted to ground to swallow her up, giving me a very confused look, and saying 'please stop, you are embarrassing me and everyone is looking'. I smiled and said 'come on let's put these toys back neatly together and we will come another day, and see if we can be nice and calm'. We walked off hand in hand smiling and eventually laughing in the car at the crazy thing I had done, with her having the final word saying 'please don't ever do that again'.

Chapter 18
Sexualised Behaviours

Many children at many ages will display what seems a sexualised behaviour, but is not always necessarily a sexualised behaviour i.e. Toddlers touching and exploring their own genital areas.

An unusual potentially sexualised behaviour that I have been witness to, was the constant gyrating, touching, 'grinding', and simulation of sexual acts by siblings, when they came into our foster family a few years ago. We reported and recorded the displays, and used the tactic of distraction, and very clear and separate 'dance' moves to allow these two little ones to express their excitable behaviours over the initial weeks. Social workers were concerned and felt they may have experienced the visual element of either pornography or their mother with a partner or partners. As we observed and discussed the possibilities, and potential reasons and danger associated with these behaviours, it became apparent that they had been subject to a 24/7 gala of MTV music videos in the company of their very young unemployed mother, that were not necessarily appropriate viewing for such young children, but were thankfully not pornographic. We were able to extend the strategy of dance in very separate areas of the room, promoting exclusive space to dance for all, with no physical interaction from others, with this, eventually, calming their excitement and need to mimic the videos that they were no longer viewing. We then taught the pair of them about the nature of physical touch and interaction between children, keeping safe and appropriate guidelines that proved tougher than expected over an elongated period, but did, eventually, revert to safer levels of understanding after, approximately, 18 months.

Obviously, there will be instances where very clear inappropriate sexualised behaviours are apparent in young people, and it is always best practice to observe, record and report, whilst keeping the young person safe and clear of potential danger from others also. We can attempt to identify why the young person is performing these behaviours, but often it is best to allow them to continue safely without demonising this behaviour initially as it is very likely keeping them calm, soothed and more balanced/able to cope, especially if a large transition has recently been forced upon them.

You must always protect everyone in the zones of contact, including the young person performing the odd or obscure sexualised behaviour, not only from immediate physical danger, but from mimicking, bullying, fun making and long term labels. These behaviours can very often be repaired or as we have seen diminish and not be present for a long period of time, although always be aware they may return at the next sign of imbalance, upset, stress or transition. Each child grows differently, and each brain behaves in its own way, depending on the pre-birth, early years, DNA, heritage and learned behaviours. Sex is a very natural human trait that is programmed into all of us, and we process it in very different ways at very different points of our childhood, youth, adolescence, early adult years and throughout our adult life. Another very important factor to be aware of is that once the sexual receptors within our brain are 'opened' within our brain and chemical make-up, they cannot be closed and will function as a very efficient part of the brain. Broken down quite simply, this means that if a child has been sexually abused at a very young age, their brain will make complete sense of the heightened feelings and chemical rush this often brings, requesting more of the same exciting feelings. We witnessed this within a young lady, whom I have mentioned in earlier sections of this book, who was sexually abused in her early school years (the perpetrator was found guilty on her evidence and was imprisoned for many years) where she would feel extremely heightened when undressed, in the bath or shower and post exercise or a thrill such as a roller coaster or even a large hump in the road. She would need to rub her genitals against something that ensured she felt the pleasure of the experience her brain told her was the correct option when adrenalin was flowing, thus we had to ensure she (aged 8 through to 16) that she had this opportunity in private, never rushing her to get dressed after swimming, for example, or instructing/allowing her to visit the toilet post thrill ride at Alton Towers. We learned this after a trip to a kids indoor play zone – of the ever popular padded scaffold type – when she hopped over a crash barrier in the car park, realising halfway that she could rub herself along the length of the smooth metal barrier gaining the pleasure she needed.

We should appraise the behaviours and attempt to address them in a sensitive but obvious manner, labelling the behaviour as it presents itself to us, helping the person to understand that it is an unusual act that not everyone participates in or understands when others do. If at all possible, allow the young person to continue the behaviour in a private area (normally their bedroom with secure door and privacy), and identify, show and describe what we would suggest is the more regular behaviour or acceptable norm in this case. Never ask why they perform such acts, just allow them to know that you are sensitive to their need, whilst keeping them and others safe. As time progresses, the behaviour may, and often does, diminish as the young person becomes more settled, comfortable, trusting and confident. If this is not the case, then we need to seek help from the professionals within our network, where the behaviours can be assessed and help given in the correct area.

We have found it very practical and rewarding to show all of the children in our care the acceptable boundaries between all people. We undertake this by physical action reminders that if we are standing, sitting, laying or present in any way in an area the personal space that we own is the space inside our outstretched arm as if an imaginary force field – boys always understand quicker than girls due to good old Star Wars and Sci-Fi stuff – is protecting us. If you wish to enter this area, you should politely ask and enter only when clearly invited, and then you must act appropriately and leave again when asked nicely, not taking offence or questioning why you have to leave. This very simple task protects everybody and we will all be grateful of its existence one day with someone. We have experienced great success with this strategy, and over time it makes interaction very comfortable and safe with all enjoying the very clear instruction and boundary.

Chapter 19
They Can Learn – They Will Learn, They Want to Learn

How do we get these children to learn?

I am often asked this question by adoptive parents of children aged between 7 through to 10, who strongly believed there children would eventually 'adopt' and mimic their traits, behaviours and learning style, ridding themselves of the understandably 'odd' or 'non-conventional' behaviours they portrayed when they were younger. These children can and will have very often been affected by many of the areas we have discussed earlier in the book, ensuring that in most cases, they cannot fully remove these from their being and behaviours.

As with any individual, it is important we find the 'code' to what makes these children 'tick', what excites their brain, where their skills lie and ultimately, change the style of teaching to suit this 'model', 'code' or 'programme'. I would strongly promote mainstream education for the majority of the children that seem 'difficult' or 'different', especially if the long term appraisal confirms that they will be very likely living a 'mainstream' adult existence. It is very important that they get to make as many mistakes as they can, learning from experiences and the consistent, continuing patterns that real life will throw at them. Every child mentioned in this publication has been in mainstream education when they have been in a learning environment i.e. some have had extended absences due to life issues, but have never attended any 'special' educational facilities.

Here are some points to ponder:-

- Patience
- Child CV
- Perseverance
- Learning Maps
- Advocate
- Communication
- External Brain
- Separate school from home (sanctuary)
- Personal Education Plan
- SEND school register

All children want to learn, can learn and will learn if they are given the correct teaching pathway to suit their style of learning, match their brain pattern, and work within the boundaries of their skill base, 'toolbag' or areas of extreme talent. We must always work to identify the areas in which a child copes, excels, enjoys, retains information, and finds learning easiest and most comfortable. The words in the list vary in terms of how we adapt these to each child, but I wanted to separate and identify them as an easy point of future reference so that you can revert back to them at any point, as you would the car manual when you can't remember the tyre pressures.

Patience and perseverance are two way elements, and relate to both 'teacher' and pupil. They also need to be related to everyone involved in the process of progressing the young person through education and to this end, I would strongly suggest that you request, if not offered the opportunity, that your child be given a Personal Education Plan (PEP) that is reviewed at least every term with your involvement and communication form home, and everyone involved, whilst opening the door to SEND registration within the school highlighting that the child has Special Educational Needs, and requires additional help and careful planning, teaching, resources, and if at possible additional funding within the Education Authority, Academy or via a Charitable Trust that may be locally or nationally available.

An advocate is a designated individual who listens to and understands the needs and the voice of the child, often speaking on their behalf to make a sensible and coherent case for issues that need to be heard or addressed. This is, in most cases, an adult, but is not always necessarily as some young people prefer other children (possibly an older one) to relate their worries and issues to. It needs to be someone they can relate to comfortably and openly, whilst trusting them to vocalise the elements they wish to be discussed, organised and either altered or introduced. It is very often a TA within an educational environment, but can be many different individuals – use your imagination and keep an open mind to opt for the most appropriate and efficient Advocate.

An 'External Brain' is quite simply someone else who assists the young persons with processing issues, aiding them to make sense of whatever they need to in terms of learning, social interaction and any area they find it difficult to make sense of. Every child with difficulties who is 'different' will benefit from an 'External Brain'. This does not need to be a single person, but can often be many people across the spectrum of everyday life, learning, education, in the playground etc. Again, 'think outside the box', and draft different individuals in to assist and coach the child and their brain in every area they are involved in. A single person cannot and should not be the 'be all and end all' for these children, as we want to explore their learning styles and capabilities as broadly as we possibly can, ensuring we have uncovered their skills, and 'specialist subjects'. Savant Autistic individuals are a great example of this as their brain patterns are extremely complex and unusual, but they will major in a very highly functioning area i.e. the mathematical processing skill of Dustin Hoffman's character in the hit movie 'Rain man', and the unbelievably skilled memory and artistic Stephen Wiltshire, who draws world architecture and the skylines of major world cities from memory in the most amazing detail, and of course, who would not have been deemed to function at any level, unless these extreme skills were unearthed.

I have found it very productive and helpful to produce a 'CV' for the children I have worked with over the years, identifying to everyone that works with them:-

- who they are
- how they learn
- what their skills are
- what they love to participate in
- where they like to sit in class
- how often they need breaks
- at what age they are functioning socially (very often ½ their chronological age)

Be inventive and ensure you update the CV each time you feel it is necessary. Ask for the year curriculum, and expected outcomes and targets, highlighting each year the elements that your child has achieved and has not achieved, ensuring teaching staff (who change) know where the 'gaps' are in the child's education prior to attempting more complex areas of the subject.

Personally, I feel very strongly that 'what happens in school stays in school' and vice versa. It is important that the child is allowed to make mistakes, fail, feel imbalanced and/or unhappy, anxious and angry with one, without it 'spilling over' into all of the environments. We will discuss later that punishments and sanctions often do not work, ensuring we need to work in differing ways to help the child accept the failures, put them to one side, relax and enjoy the areas they can, when they can. Nobody learns when they are miserable. To this end, never engage in 'battles' over homework and never feel it is your responsibility or a reflection upon your ability to parent a child who you cannot force to complete their external school tasks. Always give them the option and help them to organise their time, place and materials to be able to efficiently take on the task of homework, whilst clearly, but non-emotionally, pointing out to them the consequences that come with not completing your homework i.e. Possible detentions, shame in front of others if you are the only one to have not completed the task, a gap in their learning etc.

Above all, communication is the key to a successful education in whatever form this will take. With efficient discussion and liaison, the correct pathway and learning programme will be identified, and you will allow the young person to achieve to the best of their ability – and that is all we can wish for. Remind yourselves again that there is not a 'norm' in any area of the development of a human being, and that diversity is the longest word in the dictionary and it has infinite possibilities and surprises.

Finally to close this section – although I could easily and possibly should, write a complete book on strategies to educating the 'difficult' child – I have the very happy and proud knowledge that we, in conjunction with some amazing educational establishments, have managed to facilitate (with good communication and individual programmes) two young ladies with attending and successfully completing their chosen course at University, after battling early life experiences, FASD, placement breakdown at age 14, being very close to suicide at age 15 (prior to and soon after coming into care). Another young man, who could not read and write at age 11 having attended primary school for less than 1 year in total, striving through to achieve 5 GCSE exams at Grade C and above.

You can help these children to achieve, and they will work with you and the teams available if you adapt your skills and teaching styles/tools to harmonise with their abilities and capabilities.

Chapter 20
Startle Response

After that very heavy section, let's take a lighter look at why some children portray very unusual effects when 'startled', are 'startled' by some very odd stimuli, and how we can help them to regulate their responses, keeping them calm and balanced when it is possible they may 'jump out of their skin' – to name one of the more polite and usable phrases associated with this. The response creates a fear and discomfort in the victim that is very individual, and needs to be observed and understood to be able to help or progress/improve.

First of all, does your child/ren show an extreme response to loud noises or something they are not expecting? Many children who have experienced disorganised early years and in particular children with FASD, tend to respond either very quickly, and what would normally be judged as excessive/over dramatically if they hear a loud noise, see something their brains were not predicting or if something makes them jump. There is also a strong possibility that they may display no response when you would normally expect one, if startled and some have a delayed response as if it were 'shock'. When and if you had very young babies, I am sure many of you were told to 'carry on as normal and make lots of regular noise' around your sleeping baby to ensure they get used to the noises, and are not awoken by them or startled. 'It is best if you do not wrap them
in cotton wool' would often be the good old saying, and we all hovered around the child and banged the door etc. when they were tiny and asleep, programming their brains and senses as we would like them to be – balanced, level and/or

normal depending on how you describe, and what era or generation you were in. This is precisely how most babies are conditioned, and it generally seems to pan out and create regulated responses as we would expect.

How do we combat this a much older child that is still showing difficulties regulating their 'startle response'? My experience lends me to suggest 'in exactly the same way'. No matter how old someone is, they will only feel safe with what they know, expect, anticipate and understand, making sense of the incident, noise or unexpected happening in a way that is practised and learned from trusted adults, peers or other sources of comfort. To this end, it is completely up to us to train and condition the response of the child in our charge by allowing them to experience these necessary learning milestones, helping them to make sense and cope with them as often as we can. It is important that we cover all of the elements that may 'startle' a young person, and if necessary, manufacture, role play, throw in the odd 'curve ball' and really experiment with how they deal with these, ascertaining whether they require additional help in feeling safe around when faced with them.

Some areas that I have witnessed that cause unusual effects and potentially 'startle' young people are:-

- Smoke alarms
- Clock alarms
- Vehicle horns/hooters
- Dogs barking
- Someone unexpectedly 'popping up'
- A door opening and someone appearing
- 'Humps' in the road and that 'tingly tummy feeling'
- Shouting
- A door banging
- Sudden braking in a vehicle
- Insects flying near them
- Spiders

There are many others, but I am sure you get the gist of where we are going with this – it is imperative that you explore what makes the child respond in this way and not so much understand why, but deal with the healthy and rational response which hopefully you are able to show them, and maintain calmness.

Be inventive and also use any examples you can see on TV or in Movies that you watch together, allowing them to express their fears, whilst you display, and reassure the child that it is ok to have fear and demonstrate a healthy response enabling them to eventually gain trust, safe feelings, and mimic your calm and rational outcome. One way that we have investigated to understand the children's fears is to play a mock game of musical chairs with only one chair missing at any time, and whoever is central to the circle and 'chairless' names something that makes them feel fear, and describes how it makes them feel, how they react and if they think others feel the same i.e. 'spiders make me cringe, grit my teeth and say uuurrgghhh – but I know some weird people like them'. This game just creates a fun way of expressing the fears we feel, naming them and sharing them to gauge other people's feelings and responses – feel free to throw in an example that you know or suspect causes an extreme or unusual 'startle response' in a participant so that it can be specifically discussed and evaluated by all. Be careful to never allow anyone to mock others fears and be sensitive to any additional feelings or reasons for the fear being divulged, as this may well happen as young people begin to feel more comfortable and relaxed in the family, class or group. Some may be easy to alleviate and equally some make take a long time, but continue to 'test' the responses, as long as they are not dangerous or harming to the young person.

Chapter 21
Social Boundaries

Although a significant way through this book, I would suggest that the understanding of social boundaries is going to be the most difficult area for you to make any progression with when working with young people with behavioural difficulties or unusual brain patterns. The people around are so diverse, unpredictable, ever changing and confusing that it is enormously complex for anyone to make complete sense of everyone they meet and interact with, let alone a young person who has very different processing abilities, visions of themselves/others, and obscure expectations that add to the confusion and potential to progress in making sense of others.

A good start point is always at the beginning – Hello, Please, thank you, how are you?, pleased to meet you etc. along with good modelling and very clear boundaries as mentioned earlier. One exaggerated example of the 'boundary' theory is to draw a circle arm's length around you and the young person in separate areas of the patio, path, playground, hall or wherever you may be, and explain very clearly that we are not allowed to enter the circle when talking to each other, but we can offer to shake hands, offer a 'hi 5' or just simply give a little wave when saying 'hello', helping them to understand that it feels intrusive if someone enters your circle and demonstrating this to them in a humorous manner.

This will not be an area where you will see speedy progression, and I often describe the children I have worked with and look after directly as 'being in the first playground' as far as Social interaction and understanding is concerned, and that pretty much covers all of them from age 4 through to 17/18, so do not be surprised if this is the case with your young people. The only thing we can do is be patient, be proactive in putting the children in social situations and allowing them to make mistakes, explaining to them where they went wrong in a sympathetic manner. When it does go wrong, tell them how they could have succeeded, and then ask them to repeat what you said and if possible, re-enact what would be appropriate and correct to show them how it sounds, feels and plays out.

Most children with difficulties in this area will display as half of their chronological age, and as long as we know this and our expectations are linked to this knowledge, we can make sense of and cope with their behaviours. Try very hard to keep the anticipated expectation at this level, thus adjusting areas of play and social interaction to suit, predicting the obvious outcome and managing the areas, interactions, and if necessary, the people they frequent with, until you feel you can progress on towards the next age/stage of social development.

My final and most important recommendation in this area – which will prove an enormously difficult task for most of us – is to not worry if the young person does not have any friends. Often, it will be a conundrum to our young people that is beyond their capabilities and they may be able to initially appeal to many other children with either, their humour, acting out, sporting ability, musical skill or physical presence, but they will not be able to maintain the other's expectation or mimic their actions for very long. They will either 'flood' their peers with attention and necessity to engage, being excessively demanding or they will very quickly realise that they have nothing new to say, and will either be repetitious and challenging for the other young people or on occasion, just 'drift away' in total confusion as to what you do next, what can you say or why don't they want to do and say what I want to do. Do not feel emotional for the young person, as again this will be confusing, and you must allow them to continue to practice and revisit the social engagement with as many different individuals as you can to allow them to make mistakes and potentially progress, although this may be beyond them. Very often, they will not attach emotion to the interactions and failed attempts to engage or maintain friends, apart from anger which in my experience stems from the frustration of someone not understanding them, rather than them not understanding why they are different.

When a brain pattern is wired in such a way that social interactions are continually confusing or unimportant, it is important to understand that it is very likely that this cannot be significantly altered in any amount of time. This can have been caused by many issues and it is not really necessary to understand why, as this will not source the 'code' to repair or improvement in the form of an epiphany – only hard work, patience and the advice as set out above can be any measure of progression and better understanding. It is very interesting to see two very similar individuals attempt to interact socially when they both experience the issues as discussed – they find it even more difficult to bond and accept each other, repelling like magnets?. It seems they can see how everyone interacts, likes what they see, but cannot allow their actions to mimic and regulate the correct percentage of 'give and take' ensuring a successful long term friend or relationship. Protect them as you would very young children, but remind them by allowing continual interaction and appraisal with as much teaching and training as you possibly can, being very honest and open in the early secondary school years, outlining where they could improve and why things are proving difficult if frustration is apparent. Go back to the simple stages, and reiterate the importance of engagement and boundaries where necessary, and never be afraid to repeat the steps – it is very possible that each new meeting will bring the same issues and they will not be learned/transferrable to the next person or situation. Poor memory recall will of course exaggerate this, but again, do not over protect and not promote social interaction, as you may be surprised by a small progression in the most unusual guise.

Chapter 22
Speech and Language
(Communication)

A very apt progression from the previous chapter is speech and language. I was, when asked to consider this option for a young person in my care, taken aback by the extent of skills a Speech and Language professional/programme can provide over and above the obvious difficulties of stammers, stutters, lisps etc. that we place under this banner, and I think you may be too.

A professional in this area not only concentrates on speech defects or difficulties, but in a young person's ability to be able to correctly express themselves, building confidence, positivity and ultimately, self-esteem, which is the key to efficient communication and in turn, happiness. We all know how important it is to value, accept and love 'you' prior to having any success in understanding and communicating with others.

We commence confidence in speech and expression in the very early years of development, and we build success upon elements such as nursery rhymes, jokes and sometimes copying or mimicking fictional characters or role models. This can be introduced at any age and used as a confidence tool allowing the young person to repeat the necessary song, phrase or 'ditty' to try out different ways of using verbal language, experimenting with what feels most comfortable or makes them laugh, feel happy or of course, what they do not like. Work on the positives and find an area or subject that the young person feels comfortable with, letting them take the lead and expressing their personality, and if possible, their opinions and preferences.

A good working example of this that we have successfully used is facts, TV shows and commentary relating to the sport of UK Premier League Football, with a young 11 year old lad who entered our care at this age, unable to read or write, thus being very reluctant to communicate in any elongated manner, causing him anxiety and placing huge barriers in his pathway to development, not only educationally, but more importantly, socially. We were able to help him learn and develop his reading from Sky Sports News every morning at breakfast, and every evening after school, managing to convince the teaching staff at school to allow him to produce verbal reports, recounts and opinions following on to the same in written form. This young man managed to successfully complete year 7 through to 11 at mainstream school with the help of a carefully chosen balance of practical and academic subjects, not only achieving 5 GCSE at Grade C, but also securing The Principal's Award for Endeavour three years out of the five he attended. They were not smooth and calm years by any means, but the fact that we all allowed him to make sense of the world of verbal and written form in a subject area he felt in control of cemented the success and – please excuse the pun – 'cast a sturdy foundation' that he could really build upon, making complete sense of. He can now, at 21 years old complete forms, job applications, and communicate in both written and verbal forms in the necessary areas of everyday life, creating and maintaining a successful existence as an independent adult. He still struggles with social understanding and 'boundaries' but he continues to 'strive to progress' by interacting on a daily basis and making mistakes with friends, colleagues, and of course, girlfriends, regularly asking advice and confirming 'I know where I went wrong', but then adding 'she was weird'.

Movies and TV shows can be good teaching and discussion methods for improving a young person's communication skills – they are very obviously on trend with the present generation and are followed – maybe even worshipped – by young people these days. Make yourself aware of the programmes your young person regularly watches or watch them together and communicate around them – don't be silly enough to try and chat during them though! Make the viewing an experience that is shared and is very clearly a point of discussion, with mainly positive outcomes where possible. Depending on the chosen show or subject, it may be necessary to discuss the negative elements also, but attempt to be sympathetic and understanding of why it is popular within the younger generation, and 'spin' these elements into as many positives as you can creating creative and enjoyable conversation and interaction.

If you feel that the communication is becoming excessive on their part, use simple and age/ability appropriate strategies to ensure they take time to think, be quiet and focus – some examples may be chewing gum, sucking a sweet lolly, the good old tradition of eating popcorn or the 'dangling of the carrot' in the form of a reward at the end of the period of silence or reflection/allowing others to express their thoughts or opinions. It is always important as in any interaction to ensure we allow them to experience clear mandatory rules, different opinions and essentially 'confrontation' as this very much forms a large part of successful communication and will inevitably be part of their interactive experience that follows, owing to their difficulties in understanding this area in its overall entirety. Again, use role play and trusted participants to practice these areas, ensuring the young person can be accepting, understanding, calm and non-violent in their reaction.

Engage the skills of a Speech and Language professional if you have the availability, opportunity and access, as you will not be disappointed, and you, as I did, will very likely learn skills that you can utilise in many differing situations. I was very lucky to have an opportunity to liaise with a highly skilled Therapist specialising in this area – whilst working alongside Dr Valerie Dunn at Cambridge University Research Faculty on a pilot project when asked to pen the FASD insert for the impending 'Young Persons Mental Health' guidance sheets – and I have never looked back since, confidently citing on many occasions, that this is the single most productive area of Therapy I have experienced with any of the children I have looked after or been involved with externally, working alongside and/or in conjunction with their Birth/Adoptive/Foster parents, teachers, social workers or assisting professional.

Be inventive, be simple and most of all, promote as much fun and enjoyable communication as you possibly can. Allowing anyone to verbalise or express anything in any form, promotes good communication and ensures a healthy flow of interaction that will ensure progression in some form at some point in the future.

Chapter 23
Cause and Effect (Consequences)

Does your young person realise the outcome of the action they perform in all instances?

The resounding answer will not merely be a quiet 'no' – I am pretty sure it will be a scoffing, loud 'of course they don't'. This is an enormously difficult skill to master, and takes a huge amount of processing ability and conceptuality – this will not be present in many of the brains of the children and young people that struggle with the elements we have discussed so far throughout this book, and will very likely never be.

This section, although possibly not initially obvious, follows on nicely from the areas of sociability and communication that we have been discussing in the past two chapters as it is another barrier to effective and safe living with others, often highlighting quite large differences between the young people we are in charge of and working with, compared to the majority of children within society in the developed world. The world is moving at an accelerated speed each year technology advances, and the young person is being asked/must be able to 'keep up' and progress with the 'pacesetters' creating the potential 'norm' This is going to be virtually impossible for the child that cannot make sense of cause and effect in most cases, but in many, it may also be the case that they are able to cope in an enhanced capacity with this more 'black and white' medium over the complicated nature of human interaction, which is unpredictable and often nonsensical, and sometimes, even 'mystical'. Computers, mobile phones and electronic gadgets can often be much simpler for young people with 'fixed' or 'obscure', more autistic styled brain patterns, in as much as they are extremely predictable and controllable by the user only performing the instructions that are requested. To this end, use these mediums as examples of how to control and predict cause and effect in young people. It is a very simple form of helping them to understand that many elements of the world around us are in fact 'fixed' and 'predictable' if you experience both the correct and incorrect ways to interact or use them, making sense of the outcome, and recording and recalling the result for future use.

As in previous sections, the use of TV, movies or forums such as 'YouTube' and even 'You've been framed' can prove useful teaching aids for many physical examples of 'cause and effect', and keeping safe around apparatus, vehicles, rivers and other areas of potential harm or danger. The former, if carefully chosen, can also prove important teaching tools in social terms, especially 'real life' TV series and movies that the young person can relate to, highlighting character difficulties with other children, persons of authority and people in general – the obvious ones being Soap Operas, Documentaries (Educating Essex/Yorkshire etc.) or movies relating to the specific age group. Be careful to opt for recognisable subject, location and demographic areas that the young person can realistically relate to – quite often TV shows and movies from other countries do not relay well and will always be 'fantasy' to a young person who struggles with concept, lateral thinking and anything but 'how it is'.

We can use the skill of role play in this area to follow up on an area that the young person has experienced first had or viewed recently. Always ensure it is fresh in their mind before engaging in any teaching or re-enactments to maximise relevance and understanding – I made this mistake with one young lady and she just thought we were 'doing a play'. Always discuss or 'play out' what did happen, finishing with what should happen and go back to our strategy of telling them <u>what to do</u> rather than what not to do.

Chapter 24
Lies, Dishonesty and Stealing

I will start this section by confirming one very important strategy for you as an adult:-

- Do not take it personally

Perhaps, I should have printed this larger, bolder, in red ink or with flashing lights, as I cannot express strongly enough how much you need to disassociate your emotions with this area of behaviour. It is a habitual, unconscious decision in many of the young people we are relating to, aiming to help and discussing in this book, thus they do not see the problem or issue with the action and are definitely not directing it at you/wishing it to affect you in any shape or form.

Many young people could be tagged as 'Magpies' and it is very possible that 'Peter' from the famous Wolf/lies fable or fairy story, struggled in the same way that the young people we are working alongside do. It is guaranteed that you will be forced to address these areas, and attempt to help the young person make sense of and overcome the necessity of their obsession to lie, cheat or steal – maybe all of them on many occasions and on a continuing basis, depending on their ability to process and learn the concepts of honesty, truth and integrity. In my experience, this is a very regular issue with many of the young people I know respect, trust and possibly even love me, that still confuses them enormously, and proves too difficult to avoid. The lies change, the dishonesty becomes less intense, and the items they steal become smaller and in their eyes more insignificant, but they find it pretty much impossible to eradicate in its entirety.

I have many tried and tested strategies that I can relay to you – the reason they are many and tried and tested, are that they have been used on so many occasions, and have proved a success for that particular lie or stolen object, however, this does not mean they have resolved the young person's issue of lying or stealing as every new lie is a new entity and every different object stolen has a different identity to the last one, having no obvious connection that can be related to it also being an issue or wrong. You will have fun.

One strategy I like to use, is the one where as an adult you tell a blatant lie to the young person who continually offends and then wait for their reaction. When the penny drops and they make sense of what you have said, make your apology and then quickly explain why you told them a lie, concluding the discussion with the question to them 'do you think it is ok that I lied?'. This strategy can be used in connection with cheating whilst playing games – which seems also to be a regular occurrence – as long as you very quickly 'out yourself' for cheating, and make it very clear that you forfeit the game and the other player triumphs with no reaction apart from agreement. Sometimes, you have to perform this to allow the young person to see the crime and the reaction in real time, giving them the opportunity to reflect, and register the behaviour and the outcome.

As far as stealing is concerned, it is my experience that many young people feel anything that is accessible is 'fair game' and can be taken by anyone. Never punish and always ask them to return the item/s without reason or anything but a smile, explaining to them that this is someone else's property, and should not be taken unless specifically asked for and agreed to remove. You can reflect this upon them by removing items from their belongings and returning them before they become aware they are missing with the explanation that you took it, but it was not yours and you remembered that you must return it to its rightful owner – you have to be careful and know the young person very well to perform this option as it could be misconstrued by a very untrusting and confused young mind that will only take offence and/or feel it is acceptable.

If stealing becomes excessive and external (i.e. Shops, school etc.), ask a local Police Officer or PCSO to intervene, helping the young person to make sense of the consequences this behaviour will bring if undertaken. If, before you have had chance to help the young person make sense of the consequences they offend and are caught by the Police or a Store Detective – as one of my young people was on the 3rd day of placement – allow the store and/or the police to process the young person and the crime, supporting them, but not making any excuses for them, finally using the opportunity to address the serious nature of the crime, and keeping a very calm, productive outlook on the issue ensuring they respect the law and other people's property in future. The young lady in question was 14 at the time and was made to sweat a little whilst she awaited my – purposely not prompt – attendance at the shopping centre offices to process the issue and accept the warning. This worked perfectly and I was able to discuss the issue without emotion or blame, keeping the facts and the correctness of the store detective in focus – she made this the last time she offended and she respects other people's property in all instances. The importance of keeping calm and not apportioning blame is imperative, and if necessary, use the phrase 'I am guessing you did not realise this was unacceptable, but I am sure you will from now on'. As adults, we do not need to judge any further when someone has been reprimanded by another person of authority, only to support the outcome and the correct solution/action, making it very clear to the young person that we are there to support them and make their next decision a safer one – much the same as the earlier examples of school and home being very separate entities that do not need to crossover.

Chapter 25
Fair and Share

The next progression from the understanding of people's property and belongings being off limits is the ability to share with others, and be fair with others.

Sharing is very much a personal choice whereas being fair is a more tangible and clear process ensuring actions and behaviours are considering anyone else who may be affected by the process or issue. It can be important to share, but it is not mandatory and some people cannot cope with the concept, thus they should be allowed to opt out of sharing, as long as they are clearly guided and understand that if they choose this option, others will not share with them.

Sharing can be played out in sweets, money, and obvious terms of card games and regular everyday elements of our lives, and I have always used the teaching of maths and fractions to help the young person make sense of the process without feeling they are 'losing' some of their items. It is important that we express our feelings of satisfaction and pride when sharing with others, voicing clearly and precisely, ensuring the young person hears 'I feel really nice after sharing that with you and I hope you do too', and sees the facial expression of warmth and a smile. I would say in most cases, do not ask them to mimic the action, unless they are pre-school age and starting from the very beginning, instead waiting to see if they choose to follow suit and if they feel the same feeling we do when the action is complete.

In fairness terms, I would always use the word 'fair' in taking turns within a game, making it very clear that 'it is your turn and that is fair as I just had my turn'. If you feel they are in need of additional help in understanding the concept of fairness, try sharing out an item of food that you know they like – and that they know you also like – but weight the portion in your favour asking them 'does that seem fair to you?'. Correct the mistake, making the share even and voice very clearly 'now that is fair as we both have the same'.

Being fair also extends to behaviours towards others, but we will cover this in other sections in this book, as this concept is an advanced area that requires more specific interaction, being included within social and correctness items, ignoring the word 'fair' as it really confuses many of the behavioural issues. The word 'fair' is very hard to describe in terms of behaviour to a young person who is struggling to make sense of others and their surroundings – I prefer to use more concrete terms such as right and wrong to be much clearer, helping the young person make better decisions with less options. Keep it simple and concise – success will follow and repeat positive behaviours are more likely to prevail.

Chapter 26
Concepts – Time and Money

Most individuals who have any likelihood of being exposed to alcohol whilst in the womb, will find it very difficult to make sense of the 'concepts' that are time and money. Time and Money require very specific areas of the brain to be functioning very efficiently, and in my experience/within all of the publications and support group findings, this area of the brain is highly affected in 99% of all cases ensuring these prove enormously difficult, if not impossible – I look after one of the 1% diagnosed with FASD that can make sense of time, but her behaviours and traits tick 30 of the 36 boxes, and she has the facial characteristics of a typical young person affected by full FAS. This is one area that is often deemed unique to FASD by many experts, but it obviously can be apparent in Autistic individuals and young people with gaps in schooling, and early life neglect as they have been conditioned and shown the basic structure.

You can train anyone to understand the basic elements of time, but you must appreciate that it will take much longer and you will, very possibly need to concentrate on either analogue or digital (I would suggest digital as we move forward into a non-analogue world) along with breaking the elements down into extremely simple terms using the hours only and ignoring all what you have learned over the years in more detailed timings. The jargon associated with time is nonsensical to many of these children i.e. Do not go into the process of quarter to... BLA BLA BLA. Instead, use 'o'clock' with hours only being of importance, progressing very slowly towards half past and then maybe introducing 'just past... o'clock' or 'nearly... o'clock'. I have also found it very difficult with at least, two of the children I have worked with to impart the correct method of the 12 and 24 hour clock, even though they can make sense of subtracting 12. The 11 year old will very often say 'yes it is 15 o'clock', thus I will prompt her saying 'so it is afternoon as it is past 12, but how many hours past 12?' The regular answer is more likely '15' than '3', and so we continue and maybe we will crack it in the next 6 years, as we have made progression in these 6 years.

Another strategy that you can use for time, with simple instruction and involvement is with the introduction of a cooking style timer – one that twists and sets the minutes up to 60, raising an alarm when it reaches zero seems to be the most successful for us. Tell the young person they have ten minutes to complete a task or finish what they are doing i.e. Watching TV, have a shower or any area that you feel they either struggle to focus, complete the task or 'drift away' during said task or activity. Keep the minutes very short to start with and keep them consistent so that the young person starts to hopefully gauge that particular length of time – say 10 minutes. Once you feel they have grasped each task and are ready to progress, introduce longer sessions or tasks, and also throw in a little challenge to really gauge whether they have recognised this length of time and could cope without the timer perhaps.

This strategy works very well with young people with memory issues, and allows them to be more efficient and feel they are achieving and marking progress. Again, where the issues arise from is irrelevant and it is very much the element of training that young person's brain to work to the best of its ability, and be able to function and successfully progress them forward into independence.

A very basic strategy for time management, which allows the user to make complete sense of independent tasks at any age is quite simply working on the full hours and concentrating on how long it will take you to get to a place. Let me explain and make sense of this by use of an example we put into force with one of our young people.

G is 17 and starts college at 8.55am, and it takes either, 20 minutes to walk or 5 minutes on a bus if timed correctly, however, buses only run every 20 minutes and they can, of course, have issues and encounter traffic etc. G's brain only makes sense of full hours and sometimes half hour marks, but if distracted this cannot be guaranteed. The most efficient strategy for G is to leave the house at 8am whether getting the bus or walking. This is a recognisable time that G can relate to and make sense of, (wake up alarm will be set for 7am to easily ensure there is time for a shower, breakfast and getting ready) allowing the opportunity to decide whether to walk or bus it today – mostly dependent on weather, but as we are human, maybe based upon tiredness or mood. This strategy covers all the bases and it is with lots of consultation, and sometimes even the physical act of testing the route or journey that we can convince the young person to make and stick with this simple but effective strategy. It covers a nice easy 20 minute walk that will ensure arrival nice and early with time to settle and prepare – always promote settling in time and being early as this ensures calm, productive days in my experience – or even time to get a hot chocolate on the way, once this has been mastered and is comfortable. It also covers the 5 minute bus ride, whilst ensuring no real reason to run to catch the bus. It takes 5 minutes to walk to the bus stop and the bus arrives at 8.20am, thus allowing calm time waiting for the next one. If on time, the bus arrives in the City at 8.25am and a short 5 minute walk to college ensures a similar outcome to the walking option. Finally, this strategy allows for a delayed and/or a cancelled bus as G has the back-up strategy that if by 8.30am no bus has arrived, then it is time to get your walking shoes on (sorry – I should not have used that phrase as G will be asking 'which ones are my walking shoes', or 'I don't have any walking shoes, what shall I do?'), still arriving 5 minutes early. If say college or work started at 9.15am, I would still urge you to work with the full hour markers and get G out of the door at 8am, factoring in a definite stop in the City to get a coffee or a snack ensuring that the main part of the journey is resolved and completed, allowing a higher success rate. We have used this strategy extensively with at least six young people who struggled with time, and it has proven enormously successful in ensuring they arrive on time and calm, ready to learn or work. G uses this strategy in the weekly working structure, even requesting line managers schedule working hours as full hour markers – e.g. not 8.15am or 8.45am – to help maintain punctuality and efficiency, which is obviously welcomed by all and proves extremely successful.

The concept of money is pretty much identical to time in that it is very difficult to break down and teach in terms of differing coinage, pence and pounds, thus we concentrate on the pounds as again the world is much more accepting of pounds, whilst of course 'pence' will very likely be obsolete before we know it! A very intelligent young lady with FASD – who experienced early life neglect, abuse, trauma and attachment issues stemming from the necessity to be weaned off Heroine at birth – who went on to complete a degree in Journalism, joined our family age 14, and she could not make head nor tail (good pun!) of money and would regularly make mistakes in amounts, what notes were what and it seemed she had absolute disdain for the concept. I worked with her over the next two years to, eventually, train her brain to respect money and organise her brain in terms of how we earn it, spend and save it – with many mistakes along the way of course.

One very successful way of guiding her was to use the common request of 'will you pop up the shop for me please as I need some milk, bread and a pot of jam' to use one example and the process was broken down as follows:-

- we wrote a list – detailed in 4 pints milk, Hovis white sliced bread and strawberry jam
- we got her purse
- we put the list and the £5 note in her purse

She left with the instruction to pay and get a receipt, checking the change matched the number at the bottom, and putting both receipt and coins in her purse. Before she went, we also showed her the items that we needed from the cupboard and fridge so she would recognise them. She had been shopping with us many times at this point, but always became distracted. Here is an example of how that panned out across the next few days and weeks in the many trips that she made in her training:-

Attempt #1
She returned 10 minutes later with nothing and said 'the milk was 99 pounds (assuming the 'p' was for pounds) so I didn't have enough'. We discussed the concept of pence but it was impossible for her to grasp, and so I asked her to trust me and that the money was enough to cover the items. She went to walk out of the door without her purse.

Attempt #2
She returned with the correct items, very proudly in her arms but had dropped the milk and it sprung a leak – my fault I did not tell her to get a bag – but she said 'most of it is still there'. She even said she checked the list and it did not say 'bag' so she did not get one. She did not have any change or receipt. We kept calm and tried not to laugh.

Attempt #3
She returned with the change and receipt along with a whacking great smile – but no shopping and she expleted 's*#t' before she ran out of the door to thankfully retrieve the shopping from the kind assistant that had recognised how she struggled with the task. This time we did laugh and she joined in.

I am sure you get the picture. This training continued and I am really happy to say that this young lady managed to complete her degree (the Uni waived the 'C' grade GCSE maths access as she could only record at highest a 'G' grade after 3 attempts, but she did pass her functional skills level 1) managing her money very well each week for the 3 year course and she has now held down her first full time job in a communications call centre for 2 years, whilst successfully maintaining monthly rental payments on her flat that she also manages very efficiently and enjoys a good social life – as I write, she has saved £1000 towards her deposit for her first property. At worst, she loses 99p if she makes a mistake in her change, but as the years go by, she makes sense of the larger coins and can work with two fifty pence pieces making a pound, sometimes even managing to make sense of twenty pence pieces and that five of them make a full pound, if isolated and no other notes or coins are involved. Lists and prompts are still a huge part of this young ladies life, but they work, and keep her safe and able to live a healthy existence.

This is a complicated and very much 'trial and error' based area of teaching, training, sampling, practising and progression, however, do not be afraid to experiment and push the extent to which you believe the young person can cope with, clearly accepting responsibility for any failure that may occur saying in a jolly manner 'oops, that's my fault, that did not work, now let's go back to where we started and choose the right way to get there on time/complete this task/deal with this money'. Keep positive, and constantly monitor and assess both time and money areas of the young person's life whilst you are able to, building the simple strategies that end at the very basic if you feel progression has halted and the young person has reached their peak of understanding.

Chapter 27
The Last Word

I can't believe you said that – you're not bored! No, it is not the last word of this book; we still have plenty of exciting stuff to explore and strategies to add to our 'toolboxes'. Get a cup of tea if you need to and we will move on to the next stages of our journey.

In my opinion and experience, this area is one of the most difficult to master and maintain. It is almost impossible for any adult to forego the last word to a child or young person in their charge or care with a smile (not a smirk or any other expression) on their face – this is quite simply what we need to perfect. Young people who are unable to make complete sense of human interaction will not be able to understand the concept of hierarchy and will not recognise authority in many instances. This is a fact and we must build strategies to cope with this – as we will need to with challenging, tantrums, arguing and blame, which we will look at in the next few sections – if we wish to calmly and successfully aide these young people in progressing and achieving a regulated adult life.

What is your reaction when a young person decides they are going to challenge your teaching or authority by having the last word, comment or 'mumble'? Most of us will challenge this with an authoritative and sternly vocalised phrase like 'who do you think you are?' or a slightly angrier and louder 'what did you say?', and this is how we would have expected our parents, carers, teachers and people of authority to react to us when we were young if we performed this inappropriate retort. Remember the children and young people we are specifically discussing in this book have difficulties and will display very different reactions to most children, but even if they do react in the same manner (let's not forget there are oppositional and rude young people in society that do not have good reason), they are often for very different reasons and are as confusing to them as they are us.

Try an alternative calm but clear reaction such as 'oh you are having the last word are you?'. This will usually have the effect of making them silent and quite possibly cause them to stare at you – do not believe it is a glare and even if you feel it very much is, keep a calm face and follow it up with a smile or another phrase that alters the focus of the confrontation, even if it is irrelevant to what is happening or being discussed. It is very likely you will still feel the need to confront and question the action, but it is also very likely that there will be other people present and that the young person who reacted in such a manner will be feeling angry or possibly confused. This is not the optimum point to progress and help the young person make sense of why this is an unacceptable reaction to anyone at any time. This can be done in private when they are calm and by use of relaying to them what happened, what was said and how they may feel if someone wishes to challenge someone else's opinion or authority by 'having the last word'. If necessary, choose a scenario that you know they can relate to and play it out with them in the form of conversation or role play, reversing the roles, and clearly showing them what a nicer and more helpful solution would be, pointing out to them that this behaviour is viewed as others as very controlling (this is the root cause of this behaviour but may not always be recognised by the user) and confrontational, often causing emotions and anger to run high with problematic results – obviously, in whatever language you feel best works with the young person. If you have the option, set it up as a class or family teaching session, along with other strategies to practice, helping all to make sense and hopefully, throw in a small amount of humour to lighten the intensity, also showing that calmness, humour, politeness, and generally, being thoughtful around other people is preferable to negative behaviours and traits.

I am probably now stating the obvious, but I feel it is important at this point to confirm that we should never become petty or sarcastic around 'the last word' and possibly even more importantly, we should demean or poke fun at the person who has challenged our authority – this will only heighten the negative elements of the situation, causing unnecessary confrontation that will escalate out of control very quickly. Finally, try not to punish this behaviour and if you feel it necessary to react and retake the control immediately, use, in as calm a voice as possible, the instruction 'let's discuss this further later, thank you for your input and do we all know what it is we have to do next?'.

Chapter 28
Arguing

A famous quote by the author Mark Twain starts this section perfectly:-

'Never argue with stupid people, they will drag you down to their level and beat you with experience.'

This is not a demeaning quote by any means and feel free to replace the word stupid with whatever word you feel most apt for your young person, people or maybe even a friend or family member, as it is not only restricted to young people, but very much life in general. In its broader scope, it does help us to make sense of the nonsensical nature of arguing with someone that is on a different level to you or 'speaks a different language', metaphorically speaking in terms of their brain being very much wired in an alternative processing arrangement, causing an inability to always make sense, and agree with more traditional and recognised reasoning or instruction.

Always de-escalate a potential 'argument' by use of slow, calmly toned language along the lines of 'ok… let's talk about this in a sensible manner' or defer the discussion to another time by clearly, but calmly voicing 'let's reflect on this when we have taken time to think to save any anger'.

One very successful strategy I employed to deal with a very argumentative 16 year old, was to clearly advise her that I would not engage in verbal battle about any subject, confirming to her that I would calmly consider any issues she had if she took the time to make sense of them and write them down, stating that I would happily accept swear words if this helped her express her anger. She would scribble away and the pen looked like it may set fire to the page at points, but I ensured everyone else in the household ignored her and did not comment or ridicule her whilst, very often we relaxed and watched TV together. When she was satisfied with her offer – mostly after 4 or 5 screwed up and unsuccessful attempts to express her point/argument – I would read, consider, reflect and then I would reply on a separate piece of paper restraining myself from any verbal communication at this point. This process allowed the young lady to get her point across with sense and feeling, without becoming distracted, and misguided by her anger and her foul language that would 'cloud' what she really wanted to say or express/make sense of. It was very often an area of confusion that was causing her angst and anxiety leading to her outburst of anger and confrontational actions, and by forcing her to take time to write and reflect on the issue we always – yes always – resolved the issue calmly and sensibly, helping her to understand the necessary points and learn from them. We would eventually verbally discuss the outcome, making further sense of any situation or misconception, once the issue was seemingly resolved in the written exchanges. I am pleased to say that this young lady is now 24 years old and we laugh about the 'silent arguments' that we used to have, but reflect on how successful they were, allowing us both to express our reasoned opinions more thoughtfully and sensibly, ensuring we communicated them correctly and without emotion that would have, most definitely caused more intense confrontation.

This is just one example of how you could 'tackle' the very difficult subject of arguing with young people, maintaining a dignified and calm approach without either diminishing the importance of what they need to express or quite simply 'pulling rank'. This can never work in the long term as it builds barriers to very important communication and areas of discussion that are necessary to engage in, but need to be thoughtfully considered and relayed, and explained to our young people in terms that they can make sense of, depending on where they are presently 'sitting' within their development pathway, or what their brain pattern can cope with.

If you feel you need further help to address this area of communication, I would strongly suggest a 'de-escalation techniques' course that will quite possibly be run by your local authority within the educational or social services departments for Teachers or Social Workers, Care Workers, Foster Carers and Adopters respectively. I have attended several, and have benefitted from the interaction, experimentation and practice these course/workshops provide and allow.

Chapter 29
Tantrums – Time Out vs Time In

You will have experienced tantrums in some shape or form with a child previously and it is a sometimes understandable response, although in many cases, we will observe and think 'how did that warrant this extreme reaction?'. I have experienced tantrums in differing shapes and forms displayed and 'acted out' by young people ranging from 18 months old through to 23 years old, and that is not an exaggeration – some of you may be able to top 23!

A tantrum is described in the Oxford English Dictionary as:-

Tantrum – noun: an uncontrolled outburst of anger and frustration, typically in a young child.
"He has temper tantrums if he can't get his own way."

> *Synonyms:*
> *fit of temper, fit of rage, outburst, flare-up,*
> *blow-up, frenzy, mood, huff, scene*

I would suggest that a tantrum is performed when someone does not get what they want or predicted that they were going to get when asking, requesting or demanding said item. It often, in my experience, stems from confusion and a lack of understanding, similar to the discussions we had earlier in the cause and effect', the more recent sections of confrontation, and sometimes cannot be controlled, quite simply because that individual is unable to make a reasoned appraisal or make sense of why the outcome was very different to how it had 'played out' in their mind prior to making the request. This explains why toddlers have tantrums – they are still learning, and are naïve in the sense of rules and boundaries – and we understand and more often than not maintain a calm approach, sympathetically helping them to make sense of, learn how to react correctly in future, without feeling the urge to punish them.

How about we use this sympathetic approach to all people displaying a behaviour that falls within this category, being described as any of the terms in the meaning shown above? Talk gently when approaching a young person who is mid-tantrum, and picture them as a toddler in need of teaching and calm explanation. Allow them to display anger in the form of trashing or banging around, as long as they are safe and will not harm themselves or another individual – toys can be replaced and can be used as very as extremely positive tools for promoting the understanding of money, replacement, patience, and most of a harsh but fair lesson in cause and effect i.e. Reassure the young person that it is ok that they trashed their favourite toy, gadget or personal item, but when calm, explain to them that it will be replaced at their cost, when enough pocket money has been accrued. If this is a repeat performance and it is early days in your relationship/working with this young person, make old toys, gadgets or items available that they can trash and damage safely, explaining that it is an item that can be disposed of afterwards, whilst ensuring they understand that it is still unacceptable behaviour, and 'we will work together to improve it'.

Whilst a young person is mid-tantrum, it is best to acknowledge the actions and to keep a watchful eye that they are aware of – I say 'that is ok that you are screaming/trashing, but I am checking you are safe'. A 12 year old lad who used to have uncontrollable bouts of anger that resulted in trashing tantrums in his bedroom would react very well to me popping my head into his room and calmly using the above phrase to which I would also add 'I will wait until you have finished and then why don't we have a cup of tea, and I will help you tidy up so that your room feels better when you go to bed later'. I used this strategy on four occasions with this young man and each time I intervened with this instruction, it resulted in a speedier end to the tantrum, thus causing less damage and upheaval. It started with bunk beds being pulled out of fixings on the wall and mattresses being strewn across the room, with much less serious consequences after the fourth occasion, with only a chest of drawers being taken apart, but not broken. At the point where I felt I could possibly help him make sense of this behaviour, I expressed to him that I felt we could use a different strategy to release the anger that he felt using a punch bag and a box of old toys that could be thrown away. He eventually calmed to a very sensible level and he started to use exercise as his strategy for releasing anger, going running or kicking a football up against the garage wall a thousand times.

Another workable strategy is to video the behaviour on your mobile phone, showing it back to the young person when they are sufficiently calm – I found it best the next day or two after – and simply asking them how they felt. This resulted in mostly cringes and embarrassment with them voicing 'I feel stupid' allowing you to ask again by clarifying 'no, I meant how did you feel when you were reacting like you did in the video?'. This will spark discussion and will allow them to reflect without feeling shame or embarrassment as you will not in any way be deemed to be judging them, only dealing with the facts and the actual behaviour that was recorded and played back to them.

Time-in is a phrase that many of you may not recognise, but you would, I expect all know what 'time-out' is. Very simply, 'Time-out' is usually a place away from others – a step, a corner, a bean bag, or a chair – where children are asked to sit quietly and reflect for the agreed time of a few minutes depending on the intensity of their incorrect or unacceptable behaviour and/or their progression within the behavioural programme that has been set by the adult for them individually. This strategy isolates the young person and works on the basis of quiet reflection prior to re-joining the group or activity they were involved in when the behaviour was recognised and needed to be changed.

Some children, in particular the ones that have experienced early life trauma, neglect or abuse cannot cope with isolation and the rejection can be enormously harmful to them, their mental health, and their want to trust and respect the adult isolating them, damaging any potential relationship that the adult is most likely to be attempting to build. 'Time-in' is the answer to this conundrum and it works on the same positive principles as 'time-out' except it removes the element of isolation. 'Time-in' asks the young person to join us in an area very close to where we are situated, to sit quietly and reflect upon the issue we have flagged up as being inappropriate or incorrect for a short amount of time. You will be able to gauge the positive nature of this strategy very quickly as most young people who have experienced this early life trauma respond more favourably to isolation, sitting calmly, and enjoying the closeness and safety of the adult who is taking positive steps to include them and help them reach a calmer state. This will build a full and trusting relationship much more efficiently with a stronger foundation when working with such children. If they fight to be included and want to get away, then 'time-out' may be the correct strategy, but only trial and error will confirm the most efficient method.

A sibling pair who joined our family on their first Foster placement from birth mother when they were aged 4 and 5 both required strong and consistent intervention. Their behaviours were very extreme, and early life had been traumatic with clear signs of neglect and abuse along with drug, alcohol and domestic violence issues. The younger, less emotional young lady (later diagnosed with FASD and significant memory issues) required the 'time-out' version of this method of reflection, whereas the slightly older boy very much preferred 'time-in' as he needed an 'arm' around him to help him feel safe and wanted. We did 'throw in the curve ball' and experiment using both methods for both children – it was amazing to see how inappropriate the incorrect strategy was and the significant results, within seconds, proving that each child needed to be aided to reflect in the opposite way, even though they were potentially displaying the same challenging and incorrect behaviour. We were very lucky to have such a clear example of the two methods in action, being able to evaluate each method individually and in respect of two very close in age siblings coming into care at a young age. These two children do still reside with us 6 years on, and both are doing amazingly well, working within their very individual and specific areas of strength – it is an absolute pleasure and an honour to be able to experience this progress and comfort, aiding two amazing young people in their pathway to adulthood.

There are, of course, other parenting strategies that are commonly used, but in my experience it is safer to keep guidance very consistent and simple to predict. It can 'throw' young people with difficulties completely off balance if you have an 'arsenal' of strategies to deal with incorrect behaviours that cannot be understood or recognised easily. We must be easy to read at all times, allowing the young person to gain safety and comfort from knowing the potential outcome. This again builds trust and forges relationships to grow stronger more efficiently.

Chapter 30
I Don't Know

'I don't know' is generally recognised as an unacceptable reply to any question that an adult asks a child. Most adults what answer they expect from the young person they are addressing as they want them to explain why they performed this unacceptable or incorrect behaviour that we are now questioning.

You can now read the paragraph above again and with a quick snap of your fingers wipe it from your memory. You will not require this information ever again. It is complete nonsense in respect of the children we are discussing and building strategies to progress.

If a young person with processing or emotional difficulties replies 'I don't know' to a question asked by an adult in respect of something they have incorrectly performed, it is a genuine answer and quite simply means 'I have not been able to process this unexpected question quickly enough to answer you' or 'I cannot find the answer in my brain'. Following this reply, most adults will ask the same question, repeatedly and often at higher volume each time, until they receive an answer that I estimate in 99% of cases will be incorrect, manufactured, forced or nonsensical, with quite a large percentage of the outcomes resulting in unnecessary confrontation, arguing, shouting, tears and maybe even a tantrum to completely divert the subject – it is very likely they cannot even understand the question or have become overwhelmed, very often forgetting what the question and original issue even pertained to.

Rather than ask 'why did you...', try asking a different style of question if possible i.e. A closed question requiring only a simple 'yes' or 'no', however, you may still receive the 'I don't know' reply. I could cite at least one hundred 'I don't know' replies from the children I have worked closely with in all guises and my answer to them is always:-

'I know you don't – and that is ok'

This can then be followed up by (if you feel the young person is capable and 'in the mood') 'let's try and work out why, by taking time to think'. In most cases, this calm retort will deflate any heightened tension, emotion or anger, and the young person will recognise you are being reasonable and understanding.

It is OK to not know the answer to a question, especially if it is asking why you performed an action that you possibly did not understand would be the outcome. This is very often the case with the young people we

are working alongside and it is our duty to help them to understand that it is acceptable to need time to think, require additional help understanding or just a different perspective from another person that can either logically or objectively guide them, keep them safe, help them make sense of themselves and others.

You will hear an enormous amount of 'I don't know' replies and you will not always remember to ask every question in such a way that it can be clear and understood by these young people, thus I would urge you to practice this strategy and accept it as an efficient and reflective tool that aides communication, calmness (on both sides) and enhances trust and teaching. This is without doubt one of my favourite 'weapons' and it makes me feel a huge sense of satisfaction every time I am able to employ it.

Chapter 31
Echolalia

To continue the theme of more unusual elements relating difficulties you may experience in the young person displaying obscure behaviours and brain patterns, we are going to investigate the practice of echolalia. This is the term used when someone 'mouths' or attempts to mimic or predict what you are saying as you are saying it or very soon after. Toddlers use this method to learn speech in a positive manner and we have all been embarrassed at least once by our 'little angel' repeating something we, perhaps, should have thought and not said out loud in their presence! It is a recognised skill that is an important part of speech and language development in toddlers, and we use it without even realising it in teaching methods, nursery rhymes, hymns, prayers, and the very early words such as 'Mumma' and 'Dadda' which we perform millions of times over, facing our young one desperately trying to get them to say our 'tag' first – come on, you lot, admit it and smile knowingly.

Young people who have processing delays, and perhaps, find it difficult to make sense of conversation and interaction with others will continue to watch your lips when you speak and you will find them moving their lips as if they are attempting to beat you to the words – sometimes it may feel they are mocking you or performing the very annoying 'parrot' trick. Be sympathetic to this behaviour as it is quite simply an extension of the strategy Toddlers use, and I have experienced this in at least three young people between the age of 14 and 17 as they attempted to make sense of social interaction, concentrating on how I performed this action. We take it for granted that we are able to speak fluently and make sense of how verbal social interaction works, but please treat this behaviour as if you were guiding a young person who was learning English as their second language, as often these young people are adding to their basic vocabulary and knowledge of language that is limited for whatever reason.

If you work with a young person who is obviously using this strategy, kindly ask them if they would like you to repeat any of what you said. Equally, to help the young person progress, ask them to repeat the question, phrase or instruction you aimed at them, allowing them even longer to process, and giving them the reinforcement of hearing, speaking and hearing again – this is how we learn and perfect foreign languages at school, and also reverting back to 'basics', how we help Toddlers to form speech and experiment with language. Instruct the young person who uses the strategy to feel confident in asking others they may encounter to repeat any instruction, request or part of a conversation they need time to process, never being afraid to ask if they could explain further to help them understand.

This trait may cause confusion from other peers or people that the young person encounters, and many may feel it is an inappropriate behaviour, especially in older children/young adults, causing confrontation and possibly an angry reaction as someone may see this as ridicule or an attempt to sarcastically mimic. Attempt to guide the young person by asking them to observe themselves in the mirror performing the action, and reassure them it is an acceptable behaviour with people that you trust and are helping you i.e. Teachers and professionals, but would be best not used with people who you do not know well enough or do not trust. Some may not be able to regulate their use of this strategy, thus it may cause concern and negative reaction, but eventually, as they become more confident and skilled it will diminish – possibly returning when they are either tired or perhaps feeling nervous.

Chapter 32
Shame – The Acceptance of Blame

Nice little start to a poem I hear you say. Unfortunately, there is nothing poetic about the feelings a young person experiences when this trait is high on their list of behaviours and it is very challenging to cope with, as an adult directly working with any young person who is burdened with this consistent effect of trauma.

The young person that is displaying this behaviour, finding it extremely difficult, if not impossible to accept blame or responsibility for their actions mostly believe they are to blame for much deeper issues, and their overwhelming feelings about themselves are usually along the lines of ugly, inferior, stupid, unpopular, not liked, hated, bad and very much all of the negatives tags you could attach to a person. This very often also displays in the form of extreme paranoia, with constant worry about who is looking at them, who is talking about them, am I going to make a mistake and look stupid, and so on.

One of the most difficult areas in dealing with this behaviour is that when it manifests itself in any form of negativity, it is virtually impossible to say anything that will allow the young person to revert back to calm, common sense and realistic thought patterns. As you attempt to reassure them, they will dig deeper into their negative thoughts and if you decide to use positive affirmations such as 'you are a good person' or 'You are beautiful', they will very quickly retort 'no I am not – I am bad/ugly' and this will exacerbate the feeling in the negative, as they have the opportunity to punish themselves. If you make the decision to take the alternative route and say 'you are not bad' or 'you are not ugly', they equally accept this as the negative and will reply 'yes I am – you know I am', again dipping in mood and needing to take the more damaging path.

'What do we do?'

I have found that the most productive and positive route is to allow the young person to dwell in this negative area for as long as they need to and I have learned – with one young lady who is the second eldest of multiple siblings in care, who has lived with our family for a few years now, following previous long term placement breakdowns (initiated by her controlling and violent behaviour), and early life experiences before the age of 7 when she was taken into care after some very violent, abusive, neglectful and dangerous behaviours from both birth parents and their wider family network – that the best way to accept and allow this is to say 'I can see you are not feeling at your best at the moment, so I am going to give you some space and time on your own, but will check you are safe'.

This young lady becomes enormously angry and violent on a regular basis, and she looks to apportion blame to someone else in all instances, escalating her behaviours to a heightened level that sends her into a frenzied state, with the extreme need to verbally and sometimes, physically attack that person – or sometimes a random person, who happens to be in the wrong place at the wrong time if she has not managed to find the right person to justifiably (in her mind) blame. I have known her take 3 whole days to return to being calm enough to address and discuss the issue with us. It is always with regard to something that she has made a mistake in but as she is unable to accept this, she must divert this negative element to another person and there is no way she will release this feeling until she has accepted that she may have been hasty, wrong, incorrect or sometimes just that she can 'give in', but not voice the fact that she is to blame for what happened.

It does not help that she struggles to regulate and understand 'Cause and Effect' or consequences, thus some of the issues are repeat offences, with different individuals, and other issues are much greater and more mature in their intensity, in her attempt to be liked, accepted, 'cool', 'popular', 'followed' or whatever the young people crave in this current era. We always discuss the outcome and guide her to think, but not necessarily verbalise 'who was really to blame', 'what caused the issue', 'how could you have acted or reacted differently' and 'if it happens again how will you deal with it?'. These questions and thoughts allow her to reflect but not accept any blame, unless she wants to, where she will become tearful, show embarrassment, and we always promote saying 'thank you' in preference to 'sorry', attaching 'for helping me', 'for leaving me' or 'for understanding me'.

Always reassure the young person by showing them that you are happy to make mistakes and voice that you accept this was your fault, confirming that everyone makes mistakes, and that is how we learn and progress. Use heroes, idols or role models that you feel they look up to and follow, citing how hard they must have worked, what mistakes they have made and overcome along the way. Many of our musical heroes, sporting legends and starts of the screen have made an abundance of mistakes along the way, and we must point out to the young person that people do forgive and forget, and that there are no two individuals the same, with no single person being anywhere near 'perfect'. Today's society, pressures and constant images on social media, and the likes do not help these young people make sense of the acceptability of mistakes and 'not being perfect', but I am sure you can find some examples that will help you to help them, based upon who they aspire to be.

I do not expect that I will resolve the issue completely for the young lady I cited in the previous example, as I know she will make many different mistakes in her adolescence and as a young adult, to which she will not be able to accept responsibility for. I can, however, provide the platform to coping with these extreme feelings by being consistent and progressing the method of 'taking yourself away' until you feel calm enough to face the world. We have progressed this strategy slightly with the introduction of 'when you feel down, immerse yourself in the world that you do like', thus she makes the decision to 'lock herself away' and watch continual episodes of TV programmes or movies that make her happy. This would possibly be unhealthy in many other instances, but we feel that space and time heal this particular young lady, whilst TV or movies distract her enough to not dwell too intensely upon the matter that is causing so much pain and disturbance. We regularly 'pop our head in the door', and take her drinks and snacks, ensuring she is safe – sometimes she can accept them and sometimes she cannot, depending at what stage she has reached in her very individual and personal healing or calming process.

It is important to not take these behaviours personally as they will most likely direct their blame and anger at someone they trust, and feel safe with – very possibly this is you. I am always happy to accept this, as it is a better alternative than her expressing herself and her feelings towards a more vulnerable individual and/or herself, and I am able to accept there is an element of trust. We do laugh at the actions and reactions she displays together on occasion, and although she can see that they are extreme, unnecessary and inappropriate, it by no means suggests that when she reaches that 'heightened' level again that she will be able to assess, regulate and stop herself performing this very regular behaviour. Each new situation and mistake – even if it is the same mistake but directed at or involving a new person – brings its own intense reaction from this particular individual, who seems to be consistently 'at war with her feelings and ego', and we can only deal with the next instance as it presents itself, quickly instigating the strategy that keeps everyone safe, hoping that the next time it's power will diminish slightly.

This particular behaviour highlights to me that we cannot always 'repair' people, feelings and situations, but that sometimes we have to accept that we can only help these young people 'simmer and not boil over' at certain points, periods of time of in particular instances. Our role needs to always be assessed, evaluated and progressed, but sometimes we may need to simplify, and revert back to the basic elements of our duty of care and teaching, which are to maintain a safe environment at all times, allow privacy where appropriate, to promote independence and to help young people make good decisions/understand they have a choice. This can be frustrating, when you are so keen to progress and help someone else, but be patient, be safe and be positive in the thought that if you maintain consistent good practice, you are doing your best and this is all that can be achieved. Sometimes good practice and teaching will not show immediate results, but people build on good foundations at differing speeds and understanding – it will manifest positive outcomes, and hopefully, you will see the evidence present itself eventually. I can proudly say I have.

Chapter 33
Self-Harm and Suicidal Thoughts/Actions

A huge negative and concern with this trait is the potentially and progressive element that is self-harm. When you can eventually manage to help the person – with the 'hands off' approach – it is very likely they will enter into the very dangerous decision to self-harm, or wish to hurt themselves as a punishment. I am not in any position to guide on this most complicated, psychological and potentially life threatening area, and can only advise that you seek immediate medical and psychological help by taking the young person to their GP or Accident and Emergency Department if actual harm has been self-inflicted.

You can only ensure a young person in your care, who is choosing to self-harm, is given the best advice on health, hygiene, best practice in treating wounds, and where possible, it is best to ensure that all possible 'sharps' and potential 'poisons' are kept from their reach. Always be vigilant and advise the young person that you are keeping them safe, and that you cannot make any decisions based on their health and welfare, over and above medical professional advice and guidelines.

Be very aware of potential harmful objects that may include, but not be restricted to, knives, scissors, razors, nail files, nail clippers, blades from simple objects such as pencil sharpeners, thin metal surrounds from make-up brushes or similar, items included in maths sets – we experienced one young lady who was struggling with her emotions ready to harm herself with plastic set squares that she had carefully snapped and made extremely sharp – wooden lolly/popsicle sticks can be sharpened, as can plastic items if sanded or rubbed on course paving stones. You may need to check bags that the young person uses regularly, along with coat pockets and under pillows/in pillow cases.

The young people we are working with are susceptible to the concern of self-harm and harmful behaviours as they are vulnerable, easily influenced, often mentally and socially unstable, lacking good understanding of consequences, whilst quite possibly not possessing the most likely pain responses that would be expected. Do not take any risk at all with young people who you feel could be self-harming as it escalates very quickly, and you will be helping them enormously and in the most appropriate manner by engaging professional help at the earliest opportunity.

Chapter 34
Worry Books

For the younger child, or possibly even for a teenager/young adult that feels comfortable with it, you can make use of a small note book that is utilised by the young person in whenever they feel the necessity to express a thought or feeling that they feel cannot be said and heard by others. The book is usually agreed to be in the young person's presence at all times, kept in a safe place, and I have found that notepads with serrated and removable pages are best. This allows the young person to write and destroy anything that they felt they may wish to share, but then changed their mind or did not express in the way they wanted to, whilst also allowing them to tear out and either destroy or 'archive' notes that they have shared, but now wish to forget or class as complete.

When the young person has made an entry they wish to share, they can leave the book in a pre-agreed location – usually out of sight of other young people in the household, classroom or building – for their chosen advocate or trusted adult to read. It is entirely their choice whether they wish to engage in further discussion on the subject or issue they have recorded, but you must make them aware that if, in any way this action or words could be deemed to suggest harm to anyone in any shape or form, that you will have to alert the necessary professional, ensuring safety and conformation with the law.

The worry books – and even soft toys with notelets and zippable mouths for the younger children – that we have distributed to all of the young people in our care, have proven extremely worthwhile and we have been able to prevent the commencement of self-harm in two youngsters, along with allowing another to 'voice' her need to attempt suicide in her book, which we gained help for and helped her to take an alternative pathway to releasing her anxieties, worries, issues and deep lying guilt that she could not work out how to rid herself of.

Chapter 35
Male vs Female

Let the battle commence!

Only joking. This section aims to discuss and detail the fact that some children with past negative experiences involving a male or female role model/s will very likely display mistrust, and a lack of respect for this particular gender as a whole. Many young people have experienced being 'let down' by a parent or adult that is a supposed role model and some have experienced a particular person of either gender displaying clear weakness, unfortunately often physical, that effects their ability to view this gender as able to keep them safe on a very basic level, which is the 'level' many of these children will be working upon.

It will very likely be the very basic, ancient stereotypical model of male and female that these children understand, thus they will often challenge the female role, believing they cannot keep them safe as they are physically weaker, whilst being scared of the male gender as they are violent or 'strong'.

It is an understandable reasoning and learned behaviour based upon experience and unfortunate teaching. It is also a very likely situation that the young people we are working with, have never experienced a male role model as, of course, many families in areas where children are removed from home are single parent families with either non-existent or distant fathers, grandfathers or 'uncles', thus the role of the male gender causes confusion and many issues.

In the opposite sense, we can use the necessary male and female role models around the world to help the young person understand that both men and women can be strong, authoritative, successful, and caring in equal quantities, along with, of course, displaying them outwardly to the young person within the settings we experience together. Draw on the strength of the many male and female teachers, head teachers, nurses, doctors, politicians, prime ministers, and of course, Kings and Queens throughout history that the young person is aware of, or can relate to, showing them the necessary skills, empathy and strength that are very clear and apparent in whichever way you feel best suits the particular areas that the young person requires reassurance, and further assistance in making sense of.

These examples and teachings should also cover the areas of acceptable and unacceptable behaviours between genders, and this is quite possibly best explained by use of TV programmes, newspaper or magazine articles or real life examples of both good and bad behaviours from men to women, and vice versa. It is important that we do not assume that just because the young person is not showing unusual or unacceptable behaviours towards the opposite gender, that they understand the mechanics and dynamics of a relationship, thus we would be best advised to address some of the issues that we see could be discussed – age and developmentally appropriately – in the programmes, magazines and real life situations that we know of, or come up in discussion, asking the young person to comment how they feel about this situation. Never use their families as negative or 'bad' examples of behaviour and always welcome their understanding with a phrase such as 'I can see why you think or would feel this way', following up with what is the correct behaviour, citing good examples if you are able to. Always work on the positive and ignore addressing the negative, wherever possible, as it is the good and acceptable behaviour that we wish to promote and 'lodge' in their memory bank with them ideally recalling this behaviour, and putting it into practice when the situation arises for them directly or within their network of friends and/or family.

Many relationships and placements 'break down' due to criticism and the lack of acceptance of the birth family members or relatives of a young person. We do not need to express our opinion of the family behaviour, practices or indeed crimes, and we can always easily avoid negative comments by the use of clever language and non-judgemental replies e.g. 'I cannot say whether this is right or wrong/good or bad as I am unaware of the full picture, and I find that many situations and behaviours are caused by many different factors throughout people's lives that cause them to make good or bad decisions'. Reverting back to the 'shame' session of earlier, we can also qualify that people are allowed to make mistakes and people can only really learn by making mistakes, citing that many of the most successful people or relationships have been borne out of previous mistakes.

Chapter 36
Stimuli

Never be surprised at what can stimulate excessive emotions, feelings, fears, thoughts, anxieties or unknown terrors in a young person who is displaying difficult and obscure behavioural patterns.

A smell that reminds them of darker days, a taste that brings back harrowing memories, an insect that instils extreme fear, even if they cannot recall why on many occasions – the subliminal mind can also be a very powerful barrier to progression and calm living. Some children cannot cope with particular fabrics on their skin, feel that a label in their clothing is like a dagger in the back of their neck or flank, loud noises cause them to screech and shake dramatically, and the feeling of a slippery, slimy food going down their throat send them into panic and immediate regurgitation. On first witnessing these reactions, you will feel they are excessive, over dramatic and quite often attention seeking, but take a step back and assess what is happening to the young person's brain at this juncture and behaviour. Would they wish to react in this extreme manner and stress themselves unnecessarily? No, of course, they wouldn't as they hate to be off balance and feel out of control – control is absolutely necessary in this young person's existence as we have learned in all of the sections of this book.

The odd and extreme reactions are not learned, or caused by fear of conscious experience, they are deep areas of developmental damage, quite often neural, thus, they are as much of a shock to the young person as they are to us. Be sensitive in these situations, and following these reactions carefully attempting to work out what has caused the behaviour and how you can alleviate a repeat of the issue – by ensuring the offending label, smell, taste or noise is quickly removed, and reassuring the young person that they can be calm and feel balanced again. You can only recognise these behaviours when they arise – they will be very obscure, but they will be very real and of huge concern to the young person experiencing the feeling, and often frenzied behaviour that seems to be out of their control.

Much simpler and lower level stimuli that can cause disruption to a young person's brain, sleep, focus and concentration are elements such as night lights, ticking clocks, the 'hum' of a fridge in a caravan, wall posters, 'busy' wallpaper, patterned duvet covers, wearing a watch, air fresheners, laundry aromas, bed linen materials, and anything they may complain about. Their senses are often heightened in one area and are, therefore, much lesser in another or sometimes all other areas. Do not assume as because they have excellent hearing that they can also see efficiently or taste correctly for example. Be kind to the young person and do not challenge them with phrases like 'don't be silly, it's only a…'. It will, on most occasions, not be an exaggeration, and will be causing the young person huge concern and disruption of their senses, affecting their ability to feel calm, in control and balanced. Do your best to remove all such stimuli – even if their bedroom, workspace or recreation area ends up looking like a very drab prison cell. Record and report why you have made the changes, and note the improvements that have become apparent upon de-cluttering the young person's over stimulated environment.

One of the young ladies I have mentioned a few times throughout these texts is now in complete control of her own environment, and she chooses to have minimal decoration and clutter, managing the physical areas of her life in such a way that she maintains calmness and relaxation for herself at all times. She sometimes forgets and makes a mistake – e.g. Adding Christmas lights, and different aromas to her rooms and spaces – but she very quickly recognises that this is not conducive to good sleep, feeling settled, balanced and controlled, thus removing them very quickly, and promising herself she will not make this mistake again. She will but it is a minor faux pas and generally, she knows how to promote the necessary balance in personal surroundings.

Chapter 37
We Must Change

I did consider adding this section after each chapter, as it is really the main purpose of this book, being very much the sole reason I felt I needed to put pen to paper, and challenge the predictable 'norm' or 'standard' parenting, teaching, guiding, moulding and whatever other words/methods we associate with the many ways adults interact with young people in their pathway of progression, facilitating maturity and enhancing their development, ultimately, promoting independence, resulting in a healthy, safe and prosperous adulthood.

We must, as adults working with developing young people with 'different' – notice I have dropped the 'difficult' tag – behavioural maps, strive to remain flexible, innovative, explorative, and we must always remain open to attempt new strategies, take calculated risks and extend our limits to enhance the young person's skill set, maximising their opportunity to explore their individual abilities and their extremely unique brain pattern. The 'traditional' methods will very likely fail in developing such young people, missing an opportunity to promote individual growth and success. Never be afraid to make mistakes as an adult involved with these young people, as we can always retrace our steps and quite simply 'start again'.

There is no 'fixed' strategy or template that we can apply to young people 'across the board' and each particular toddler, child, youth, adolescent, extending through to include the young adult, is very individual, displays differing behaviours, has different reasons for these traits, and definitely requires a 'custom made' set of strategies, boundaries, guidelines and unique teaching methods to progress and make sense of 'their world'.

Each individual communicates differently, learns in very much their own way, has a unique set of strengths, skills and weaknesses, pretty much proving, confirming and questioning in every way the teaching methods that many of these individuals are being asked to conform with in mainstream schooling, family life and the supposed 'norm'. This does not mean they cannot achieve and become successful individuals.

The world is changing at a significant pace and so must we. You are one of the people who can facilitate this change in developing these strategic individual 'maps' and programmes for the young people you are involved with. It is an exciting prospect and I remain excited, proud and motivated to continue my work with these young people, their families, teachers, Social Workers and professionals whom they encounter along their pathway, who can make a difference, and can enhance their individual skills and abilities, ensuring success, satisfaction and happiness.

Chapter 38
Relaxation

And relax.

It is important that you promote methods of relaxation in young people, and it is equally important that you include relaxation in your life, if you wish to succeed in supporting and enhancing any young person's development. You cannot promote healthy progression in any one else if you are not functioning at an alert, calm level, feeling controlled and organised in every sense.

Relaxation does not always involve rest and sleep, but these are important parts to consider in the wider scope of the programme of life in general, as we need 'enough' sleep to function at an efficient level. The word 'enough' is the significant element in this sentence, as again every individual requires differing amounts of sleep and rest – we must control our own quantity and quality of sleep, along with experimenting, gauging, testing and evaluating the amount of sleep the young people we work closely with require to function at their best. Many of their worst behaviours will be exaggerated by a lack of good sleep or rest, with most of their positive behaviours diminishing also.

There are many different practices, methods and tricks to healthy relaxation. One young lady I currently look after, requires consistent amounts of chewing gum to alleviate her anxiety and need to fidget, distract, disrupt, and quite simply not be able to cope with study, learning, being with other people or maintaining focus and concentration. This is unconventional in children at school and at home, in many people's eyes but the sugar-free version that is not too damaging to her teeth and metabolism, works absolute wonders and trumps any medical drugs or therapeutic intervention that has been attempted in her previous and younger years. A huge success that allows her to enhance her learning ability with proven results in year 9 and 10 which are quite frankly unbelievable in light of this young person's previous recorded capabilities and educational projections. A simple but effective method of relaxation.

Music can be a form of relaxation for many young people who experience a struggle with silence and potentially 'their very unique thoughts'. Headphones provide privacy, comfort and minimal distraction, whilst allowing the young person to relax and quite often 'drift' into calmness. Try them – you will like them. They also provide peace and quiet for many families, classes and groups that often have to experience the more disruptive young people that struggle to cope with periods of silence, and shared group working. They are used in autistic teaching programmes for these very reasons, and have proven to be hugely successful to individuals, groups and staff. There is no reason why they cannot be utilised in absolute relaxation techniques, promoting sleep at night or when programmed/necessary in the daytime also. Many adults use this calming technique to personally aid sleep and as long as the volume is kept to a sensible, healthy level, this can be used with young people too. The use of headphones during periods of travel is very efficient and comforts young people who feel anxious when travelling or who struggle to keep themselves occupied in a vehicle, which can very often lead to disruptive behaviours – refer back to transitions section for more detail.

There are many other methods of relaxation, and you must investigate the healthiest and most productive strategy for your young people, and of course, you personally, if you are not already aware of your preferred and most efficient route to a calm and rested state. Reading, watching TV, meditation, exercise, a hobby, a craft, art, a walk in nature, star gazing, fishing and bird watching are just some examples of how people find their unique form/s of relaxation, some of which you may think some of these examples are boring, weird or quite simply, not relaxing. Some people find screaming relaxing, some find laying in a bath works for them – be inventive, if the more recognised and traditional methods do not seem to work on you or your young people then find something that does as it is very important that on a regular basis we find relaxation, which in turn replenishes our energies, recharges our batteries, and allows us to gain maximum motivation to work towards efficiently achieving the best outcome for the young person that requires our help and guidance, whilst 'arming' them with the correct strategies that they can recognise and implement in their lives moving forward.

Chapter 39
Self-Care and Protection

Extending the subject of relaxation and 'looking after you', prior to being able to promote efficient progression in another person follows the necessity that is self-care and protection. We have discussed the physical element that is protecting yourself from direct harm from a young person, but this is the more in depth element that is the 'whole' being that is you. Self-care and protection involves diet, exercise, health, wellbeing and happiness. By implementing the strategies in this book, I strongly believe you will achieve satisfaction and happiness as an adult working closely with young people that require guidance, and careful strategic programmes on their journey to success. Keep your diet balanced, maintain a healthy level of exercise, ensure you are monitoring your physical health and seeking guidance if necessary, and never be satisfied unless you feel happy. If you do not feel happy, make changes, try new things, and strive for the life that you feel is best for you and your wellbeing.

Respite from everyday practices is important, much in the same way as relaxation methods and techniques are. Never feel you are unable to take respite periods for fear of either guilt, or the feeling that nobody else can cope with this young person and you will not feel rested anyway. This is untrue, and I can speak from experience in this matter, confirming that I felt exactly these feelings and when I finally made the decision to agree to a period of respite, it was extremely therapeutic and very productive for not only me, but for everyone involved in the process of looking after, caring, teaching and being responsible for the young people. The young people loved it too, as the care, attention and thought that went into the process and logistics of the respite period, that was tailor made for 'us' worked perfectly, maintaining a distant knowing, organisation, and restful period for all.

Chapter 40
Reporting and Recording

Some of us are legally bound to record and report regularly on the young people we look after or teach, but for some of you, this will not be a mandatory expectation. I would, however, ask you all to consider the value of recording and reporting the events, successes, failures, patterns of behaviour, attempted strategies, and any significant element of your interaction with the young people you work alongside. The reason for this is quite simply to assess and evaluate the strategies and progression in a more scientific manner, evidencing how you reached the success or why you feel a strategy needed to be implemented, a method failed, analytically noting the next stage of the experiment. With written detail and well-formed notes, I have found success in identifying patterns of behaviour that can be addressed, pushed further up, or down the list of priorities, introduced new strategies, resurrected previously used strategies (as an earlier behaviour has returned), and have gained easy access to professional services based upon the very clear recordings and detail that allow others to access and understand what they are working with, and may need to strategise for a successful outcome. I regularly share my notes and 'patterns' with teaching staff at the schools the young people in my care attend, allowing them further, more in-depth insight into their actions away from education matters, which in turn could help them to introduce more positive strategies.

We are all extremely busy people and I am by no means asking you to spend hours writing up the events of each day, but do try to find an efficient method of logging your thoughts, observations and recordings for future evaluation and reference. You will have previously spent more time attempting to recall a particular event or successful strategy, possibly forgetting it completely at the optimum moment, when with clever and concise notes you could have saved, not only time, but a lot of hardship, hassle and aggravation.

The young person can directly become involved in this form of recording also, and I have always, where possible promoted this interaction, feeling that it highlights good decision making 'data' for each individual based purely upon the facts of their actions, allowing them further insight into how they display, assessing whether they wish to initiate change or they remain happy with their routines and behaviours. One very capable, but intense 16 year old young lady challenged me whilst I typed the 'Monthly Placement Report' that I produce for each young person currently placed in our family, saying 'what are you writing about me – I suppose you are telling them I am some sort of Nutter?' My response to her request was a very simple one 'Why don't you write your own report using this template and we will compare reports?' She took up the challenge after an initial short period of confusion and then the keyboard 'burst into action'. Upon comparison of our relative assessments of her behaviour/successes and failures during this month, it became consistently apparent that she felt she had behaved much worse than my assessment suggested, and her feelings were much harsher and more damning than mine – she was surprised by my appraisal and again slightly confused. When we discussed the issues in greater depth, I was able to explain to her that I could see and appreciate the troubles she faced, felt and lived at age 16, with peer pressure, trying to make sense of other people and their behaviours, reactions and actions, whilst coping with a very different brain pattern due to much early life disruption, trauma, FASD, and the constant worry of being accepted in someone else's family (which she only joined age 14) and attempting to be 'normal', 'popular', 'trendy', 'cool' or whatever the requisite current 'buzzword' was. I also was able to refer her to the previous reports, and show her that she had made significant progression and quite honestly had impressed me, allowing me to assess that she would succeed, even though she does not yet know it. She did and continues to – that instance was definitely a turning point in her self-belief and she was able to measure her progression by physically reading my notes, not, as usual, dismissing the positive words by retorting 'you are just saying that'.

I hope this allows you to see the worth of recording and reporting, and gives you the motivation to either continue, or to commence to detail the events, happenings and significant points relating to the young people you are working alongside.

Have fun, and share your notes and experiences – I can highly recommend writing your own book as I have seriously enjoyed this process, learning even more as I write and remind myself of how much fun we have.

Chapter 41
DLA/DWP

Disability Living Allowance (DLA) can be claimed from the Department of Work and Pensions for all people who require additional help in achieving daily living tasks – this will include many of the young people we work alongside and care for, thus take your time to look into the process and application. Even if you feel you do not require the monies and allowances that are allocated to such needs, consider that it may be worth 'saving' these funds for the young person when they reach independence or may be used for a holiday or activity that requires additional funds where specialist professionals either run or are part of the course team. Another good reason to assess and apply for DLA is to make the Government aware that this young person is in need of assistance, and may well still be, if they do not greatly improve into adulthood – we all read with despair the difficulties people have with accessing adult services for mental health and care provision, thus I would suggest this method ensures an early alert and continuing access that can only be an advantage in diminishing service structures.

A medical or behavioural diagnosis does not bring any advantage when applying for DLA as 'needs' are recorded and assessed purely upon the behaviours, and any help required from another in relation to these behaviours. Many adults spend many hours striving for diagnosis from medical professionals and mental health specialists attempting to achieve this 'magical' set of letters after a young person's name, only to find that it does not access any additional services, does not 'jump any queues', does not secure any additional funding, and pretty much means nothing changes, apart from the levels of frustration.

Use the behaviours as set out in the chapters of this book, along with the pull out list detailing likely 'behavioural characteristics' as a prompt for your areas of 'required help' and 'additional care' for the young people in your charge, when applying for DLA. It is there to help and assist carers of children and adults, and is not an abuse of funds, if the young person qualifies based on your honest data and assessed necessity for additional help in many different areas.

The completion of the assessment and claim will be enhanced by your reporting of events and recorded details, and can be either increased or reduced each year following an assessment of your most recent data.

Chapter 42
Work and Employment

Not always an area we can be too deeply involved in, work and employment is a necessary part of success as an adult in the current climate, and with benefits diminishing it is important that we set our young people the early task of grasping the 'concept' of work, whilst building the skills necessary to gain employment that they will be able to cope with, maintain, and hopefully, succeed and progress within. Knowing your young person is paramount in this assessment, and reflecting your summary of their skills and attributes to them is very important. It is very likely they will assess themselves very differently, and in my experience, they very often have a fantastical viewpoint and vision of how employment works citing the ease that they are likely to 'get a job' or succeed in whatever they choose.

Careers advisers are available in all schools and colleges, and of course, local Job Centres and employment agencies. Use their services to give the young people you work with scope and vision of the factual reality which jobs, roles and employment they are likely to be able to gain access to, rather than you being drawn into the 'battle' that will almost definitely ensue, if you attempt to engage in conversation and debate as to what they want to do vs what they can realistically do in the realms of the big wide world of employment.

There will very likely be limited opportunities, but there will be realistic options available. It is our role to help the young person to make sense of the reality, and if possible, become excited and accepting over these options. Continue to work on their skill base and specific areas of talent, promoting clubs and local groups to follow their 'dreams' if at possible such as Amateur Dramatic Groups, Sporting Clubs, evening classes etc. Just because they are not suitable for a particular job at the moment, does not mean they should give up their quest to achieve their 'dream' role – many individuals peak at different ages and levels, and we could list many hugely successful people within business, entertainment and the sporting world that have had their success recognised much later than the 'norm'.

Good and simple promotion of working life starts at home. Give your young people, at the youngest age you feel is safe, a role to perform regularly and consistently, somewhere along the lines of washing up, tidying a particular area, gardening, feeding your pets or something that you feel you can progress and will benefit them in making sense of the physical act of work and remuneration. Appraise and assess the role regularly, making realistic attachments to a 'real' job, and teach them how holidays, promotion, tax, expenses, uniform, productivity and time keeping are important, and will always be integral to nay employment they gain. The longer you train the young person and the more familiar they become with the process, the more likely they are to feel safe and comfortable with the realism and necessity moving into adulthood. Remember that life will often project in a very obscure way for these young people, thus they will require a much lengthier process of understanding and performance.

Be inventive, be realistic, but most of all, be consistent in your methods and application when aiding the young person in their ability to understand the vast entity that is the world of employment. Everyone can find a role that suits them and as employment trends are ever changing, we must keep up with and assess the likely areas that will 'match' the skills, capabilities and unique talents associated with each individual.

Chapter 43
Never

Never take it personally – to reiterate the earlier discussions, they do not hate you and you are not the target of their anger, emotions or frustration. Remove this feeling, and life will become easier and clearer

Never ask why – they don't know why. Return to 'I don't know', and remind yourself of the strategies that you can employ in lieu of the ancient and defunct word 'why'.

Never use open ended questions – processing abilities will be very challenging for all of these young people. Ask closed questions that only require 'yes' or 'no' replies when you want answers. If possible, direct them towards the answer you know is best for them by asking 'am I correct in saying that you...' or 'I am guessing you did that because you are feeling...'

Never criticise or be negative – manifestation of positive results is borne out of positive comments, instructions and feedback or assessment. Always find a positive in any situation or issue, even if it is an attempt at humour or diversion, like 'it could be worse, it could have been me that happened to' or 'at least no one was hurt, now we can decide how we can make sure we do this better next time'.

Never argue – remember Mark Twain's advice?

Never use physical punishment – unless trained and approved in physical restraint, it is never acceptable to use physical punishment in any form. Use the strategies in this book to find preferable techniques and methods to improve the behaviour or actions of the young person.

Never accept they cannot achieve more – you will be continually shocked how much the young person with difficulties can achieve when you start to remove, and cleanse the less positive behaviours and negative traits that are maintaining barriers to learning, progressing and improving. Use the strategies in this book that are specific to the prioritised behaviours that the young person in question requires most help in altering and deleting from their persona – the rest will follow and the sky is the limit.

Never give up – have you really tried all of the strategies and ideas we have discussed in this book? If you genuinely feel you have, go back and revisit, trying the relevant strategy again, and if you still feel, you hit the proverbial 'brick wall'. Get in touch through the blog or forum and we will attempt to gain other likely strategies that others have found success with, that may, in fact, be the answer to your conundrum. Communication is never ending and cannot be exhaustive – we can always learn more.

Never throw this book away – if you feel you have either succeeded in utilising the strategies in this book or are unable to make use of its content and ideas, pass it on to someone else within your support network or offer it to your local school or social services team to pass on to a parent, carer, teacher or suitable candidate that may benefit from some additional techniques. If you feel you can enhance the ideas and strategies in this book, please feel free to annotate and return to the writer via the publishing house – I will be producing follow up blogs, forums and workshops, updating the necessary sections, ensuring we are addressing the next set of behaviours that fall within the scope of children with difficulties and the ever changing adult strategies that prove successful, and achieve happiness and positive outcomes for all.

Chapter 44
What Happens in Vegas, Stays in Vegas

As an extension to the 'never' section, I feel it is important that confidentiality, and repercussions of actions and words are never used against the young person in future dialogue, interaction and teachings. They will never appreciate you 'dragging up' past failures, bad behaviour or mistakes and to this end, I would compel you to lock them away.

We discussed the recording and reporting agreement in the earlier section, and this is really the only time we need to relay a criminal or dangerous behaviour to a third party, but again, always be mindful that 'closure' needs to be quickly and efficiently administered. If we are to progress with positive teachings and outlooks, we need to persuade the necessary authorities that such instances of extended discussion and drawn out dialogue will not benefit the young person, and our interactive programme that is promoting these positive progressions must be respected.

The wholly inappropriate line that titles this section has been used on many occasions to secure secrecy within parties that visit the den of iniquity that is Las Vegas in Nevada, USA. No man or woman is to impart any knowledge of the usually inappropriate behaviours that are performed in this City and it was recently used in the blockbuster movie 'The Hangover', thus I felt it a light hearted lead in to the next section.

Chapter 45
Movies, TV and Well-Documented News Examples

We all have preferred and differing ways of learning, and in some cases, it is good practice to utilise the many alternative routes to making sense of and seeing various versions of the subject we wish to learn more about. Movies, TV and well documented news articles can be a welcome such alternative, and that I feel can enhance our understanding, assessment and strategy building methods within a more visual, and sometimes light hearted medium. There are many TV documentaries and news articles that can be accessed, but way too many to list, however, here is my list of movies that I have a soft spot for.

- Rainman – Autistic strategies and traits of subject and sibling carer
- The Blindside – True story of a Child in Care achieving highly
- Billy Elliott – child in poverty with talents outside the 'norm'
- 50 First Dates – young lady with memory loss building strategies to succeed
- Single White Female – harsh reality highlighting mimicking behaviours
- Harry Potter – difficult child with issues progressing through adversity
- A Beautiful Mind – true story based upon extreme skills but naïve outlook

- The Theory of Everything – the intense mind, disability, drive and skill of Stephen Hawking

All of the above could be used in communicating the way in which different individuals cope and succeed, or otherwise, with their unique set of difficulties. Many of the titles also detail the development of the people around these very 'special' or 'unusual' individuals showing their preconceived ideas, their misunderstanding and changing ability to make sense of the very different set of behaviours or skills the characters possess. I regularly watch all of these titles with fondness, and enjoy the diversity and progression within them. They all remind me that we can never sit back, relax and take any young person for granted or believe we have the perfect template to resolve this young person's issues or areas of difficulty.

I am sure you can name many more movies, and can recommend other literary titles, TV documentaries and items that have been prominent in the news. Please take a moment to add any such examples to the blog and forum for further discussion, and of course, for me to view, read or discover.

Share the appropriate examples with your young people when you feel they are able to make sense and relate to them, hopefully, prompting discussion, and sparking relative understanding and correlation with their areas of difficulty. 'Screens' are a very simple medium to access and promote in the younger generation as it is very much the lifeblood of modern day living, and an accepted 'staple' within the daily needs of this generation – use it and reap the benefits. Liken the struggles and strategies to 'live' examples relating to the young people you are working alongside, and ask them to provide their assessment of the behaviours, traits and methods/interactions shown in the movie, citing how it made them feel, what could anyone have done differently or if they feel it was enjoyable, detailing which specific parts they particularly liked.

There are also many real life examples of individuals who have conquered adversity, early life issues, conditions that would not normally promote progression and of course, an episode in life that just harms someone, affecting them mentally beyond their control. Do your own little bit of research to find appropriate examples of people across history, and in modern times that may match the profile of the issues and difficulties which your young person. It is relatively simple to access the search engines and any examples will help them to relate success with adversity, along with providing a positive message. When researching, keep an open mind, and recall and relate issues to all different areas – I found good examples in generalised teachings and everyday characters, such as David who defeated Goliath and Joseph and his brothers from the Bible, Quran and Torah stories, a local lad named Louis Rolfe (gold medal winning cyclist with cerebral palsy), and all of the competitors in the Paralympics, J.K. Rowling who overcame poverty as a young mother, Johnny Depp who as a young lad moved home 20 times, and struggled with behaviours and early adult life, Mark Wahlberg, and his drugs and alcohol addictions in his late teens due to abuse and neglect, Vincent Van Gogh succeeded against the odds of mental health issues throughout his life, Susan Boyle who, in recent years, found her skill in singing despite her Autism, and Stephen Wiltshire, a young man with acute Savant Autistic behaviours who uses his very unique brain pattern to produce the most amazing landscape and skyline Art with very little communication. You will know of many other examples without even realising you do, so dig deep, and use these references to promote discussion and make comparisons.

Chapter 46
Therapies

We continue to read many disappointing accounts of how difficult it is to access Mental Health services (CAMHS) in the UK and across the world – especially for young people. Mental Health awareness is increasing, but Governments are unable to meet demands for Therapies and Therapists for many reasons, which quite frankly would form a book, thus we will not enter this zone, and we will concentrate on the theme of our discussion so far, being 'how can we help, how can we change?' The simple answer to this is very much by being open minded, inventive and a small amount of research.

Good quality therapy can come from many alternative sources, and I have experienced a few differing schemes that offer a service through schools, local groups, local authorities and education networks such as Universities, Colleges and Charitable Trusts. Again, I must urge you to be positive and aim for these services with gusto and drive. Do not worry if you have not received a diagnosis for your young person – access the list of behaviours at the front of our book, and use these to persuade the necessary service providers that your young person needs their help, and that you are fully supportive and will work alongside the professionals to enhance their strategies, methods and techniques.

Start the process with your known education network via the school or college that your person attends and gain access to the SENCO (Special Educational Needs Coordinator) within that organisation or area. Sometimes, they may be tagged as a Disability Coordinator also, but they perform the same role by assisting vulnerable students, allowing them to access supportive services that will enhance their learning, and if necessary, their organisation skills and daily life. Each School, college and University provides this service, and they are, in my experience, excellent resources with well trained and dedicated teams.

If they are unable to help the young person directly with their particular needs, they will have knowledge of external sources that can provide a therapeutic service, and these may include Charities such as Blue Smile, DSC, Mind, Young Minds to name but a few, who are able to provide support via groups, workshops, 'one to one' and other forums dealing with specific individual issues, transitions, adversity, trauma, all building self-esteem, strategies, resilience, and long term support networks for you and your young people. We have been lucky enough to access a few of these services over the years for the children we have looked after, and cannot express enough our respect for the people and organisations that are responsible for them. Some work for some and not for others, but quite often the young person will see and appreciate that you and the organisations are 'looking out for them', and will gain a positive message just from this suggestion or initial discussions with regard to accessing such services.

Inclusion and involvement are therapies in a very simple form. Local clubs and groups are often therapeutic without the young person realising they are. We have engaged the children in our care in some potentially 'obscure' activities run by local youth clubs, religious groups and the Local Authority Inclusion Team including, Cycle maintenance, Bronze Art Award, The Duke of Edinburgh Award, Cooking Groups, Ecological groups who pick litter, clean ponds etc. and the more obvious local and national groups such as Scouts, Brownies, Rangers, sporting clubs, and youth clubs attached to either religions or local authority organisers. All of these activities can build the necessary self-esteem, resilience and social interaction skills, whilst engaging the young people in differing areas of skill, exercise and social groups – never force the young person to attend, allow them to choose when and if they wish to go, stay or leave at any point as it is important that they feel comfortable, and able to interact at their pace, which will very likely be very different to how most people perceive the 'norm'. Skills can be built in these groups also and they are not only a bonus, but a great distraction to social and personal therapy being accessed without labelling this interaction as such.

Try it, you will like it. I have enjoyed all of my 'indirect' interactions with the many different Therapists, Counsellors, Psychologists, Psychiatrists and therapeutic groups along the way – you will feel an odd anxiety initially as you sit and wait, and meet them for the first time, as you will, I can guarantee, feel as if you are the one about to be analysed and this will affect your ability to be yourself – feel confident that you are comfortable in you!

Chapter 47
Alternative Therapies

There are 'alternatives' to the more traditional form of therapy, and they can be a really useful tool for both young people and you, whilst often adding the bonus of providing an opportunity to bond, spend time together and form discussion around.

Some easy accessible, more popular Alternative Therapies that you may like to investigate and research via local sources, national bodies or quite simply by Internet Search Engine could be:-

Reiki – is a Japanese technique for stress reduction and relaxation that also promotes healing. It is administered by 'laying over hands', and is based on the idea that an unseen 'life force energy' flows through us and is what causes us to be alive. Reiki treats the whole person including body, emotions, mind and spirit creating many beneficial effects that include relaxation and feelings of peace, security, and wellbeing. Reiki is a simple, natural and safe method of spiritual healing and self-improvement that everyone can use. It creates a beneficial effect and works in conjunction with all other medical or therapeutic techniques to relieve side effects and promote recovery.

Emotional Freedom Technique (EFT or Tapping) – works to clear negative emotions or 'disruptions', and eliminate the resulting emotional response or intensity to restore emotional harmony and offer relief from physical or mental discomfort. This is done by focusing on the specific problem whilst tapping with fingers on the end points of energy meridians. The combination of sending kinetic energy to our energy system, whilst uncovering and focusing on root causes, facilitates a 'straightening out' of the energy system thereby eliminating the 'short circuit' to the body's learnt response or negative emotion.

Mindfulness Meditation – is the psychological process of bringing one's attention to experiences occurring in the present moment, which can be developed through the practice of meditation and other training. A typical meditation consists of focusing your full attention on your breath as it flows in and out of your body. Focusing on each breath in this way allows you to observe your thoughts as they arise in your mind and, little by little, to let go of struggling with them. In essence, mindfulness allows you to catch negative thought patterns before they tip you into a downward spiral. It begins the process of putting you back in control of your life.

Reflexology – is a therapeutic method of relieving pain or stress by stimulating predefined pressure points on the feet or hands of the subject with the Therapists thumbs or fingers. The pressure points connect through the nervous system (similar to acupuncture) and relate to more specific areas of the body, glands, organs or mind. It is extremely safe and works alongside any other therapy or medical intervention. Each session usually lasts between 30 and 45 minutes with included discussion and appraisal, and allows exploration of issues, worries and 'blockages' that may affect mood, behaviour or positive thinking.

Chapter 48
Further Learning

We never stop learning and can never reach a peak of intelligence where we cannot be taught more. I would definitely promote further learning in as many areas as you can possibly manage with regard to specific medical conditions, areas of mental health, strategies to cope with disorders and behaviours, and psychology and sociology matters in general.

I have, over the years, accessed additional learning streams including Autism and Brain Behavioural units via Open University (Open Degrees or Diplomas are individualised), Mental Health, Attachment Disorder and Child Behavioural studies via Futurelearn distance learning (often free courses), FASD distance learning via NOFAS and 'FASD and the Criminal Justice System via FASaware UK. Most of the UK Universities offer distance learning modules and the scope is vast, but have a look and see if there are any that you feel will enhance your ability to help the young people you are working with/likely to work with in the future and try to be proactive rather than reactive – this will not always be possible as many of us are not mind readers or Doctor Who.

Always ask the Professionals you are engaging with in different areas to suggest modules, conferences, workshops or organisations that will aide your learning and skill base. Technology allows us an enormously convenient platform to promote learning and it maximises efficiency in many instances, allowing us to access the course when we can afford the time.

I hope you do enhance your portfolio with additional learning, and if you do happen to find a worthwhile and recommended course, please share this with the other readers via our forum or blog as a nudge in the right direction from a knowledgeable or experienced source saves many minutes, maybe hours and sometimes even days of blind research.

Chapter 49
Good Reads

Some good books and papers that I have read, and can highly recommend – complimenting the subject and positivity of this book – include:-

- Happiness By Design – Paul Dolan
- Emotional and Behavioural Difficulties – Dan Hughes
- Inside I'm Hurting – Louise Bomber
- Strategies not Solutions – FASD.Alberta.ca
- Autism and Asperger Syndrome – Simon Baron-Cohen

They all offer insight into young people with difficulties, and extend our understanding of how different brain patterns and conditions can be addressed, whilst also making sense of the importance of our own wellbeing and structure.

Please take a moment to read the poem by Mary O'Dwyer. It is a personal account that she penned for her Psychoanalyst. Mary experienced many trials and traumas whilst residing in Children's homes, and in Foster Care during her childhood. She was later diagnosed with Bi-Polar Affective Disorder and she went on to work as a Psychiatric Nurse after qualifying in her early 30's in 1995. It moves me every time I read it, and reminds me of the positive input we can have, even with the sometimes limited time and access to these young people and their difficulties we actually have. Never underestimate the potential results of your care and attention.

We Built a Table

Delivered to you, I was in bits.
I had no framework, no boundaries.
You provided me with a base
That we could build upon.
I had no legs to stand on.
You propped me up and supported me;
The weight was on your shoulders.
I thought I was hard and strong
You saw through my transparency,
You uncovered my veneer;
You chiselled through my deepest layers
To the soft and pliable wood.
I was wobbling, cracking, splitting, nuts.
I wanted to bolt away.
Life seemed dark and dingy, ebony;
Blocked and never ending.
You discarded my decaying rot,
You tightened my hinges and connected my joints.
I stand firm upright unscathed.
My platform has been raised.
I now know how and where I am,
And what my function is.
I no longer stand out on a limb.
I mirror your footsteps,
Coated in a protective varnish.

Chapter 50
This Book – The Progression

It is my intention to follow up with additional texts and publications as I progress my learning and experience – this book can only ever 'scratch the surface' of the issues and difficulties our young people are presented with every day, thus it covers a tiny amount of real life and workable strategies from my very limited experience, but I hope it sparks thought, development, and gives you the incentive to share your experience too, in whichever way best suits you.

The human brain, psyche, DNA, nature, nurture, care, attention, progression, technology, environment and the never ending amount of 'factors' that affect every Human Being will continue to mould individuals in very different ways – can we ever encounter two identical Human Beings that behave in the same way based upon the inordinate number of internal and external influences? I think not. Therefore, we can never assume we have 'covered all the bases' or that a specific teaching and learning strategy will work for everyone. This excites me and I hope it excites you too.

To summarise and close this book, I would like to remind you all that we can change in the ways we approach young people in our care and learning environments, and this is inspiring and progressive, being by no means exhaustive.

Success brings satisfaction, pride, calmness, and most of all, happiness – let's make the young people we work with as happy as we possibly can, in turn promoting our own happiness and wellbeing.

We may not be able to change the world, but we can change at life of another and if everyone decides this approach is a positive and achievable option, perhaps, we can succeed in making the world a happier place – this will definitely have an ongoing effect, and will be handed down and through generations.

Remove all of the lazy terms such as 'the norm, 'regular', 'good', 'bad' etc. and exchange them for positive strategies that allow us to work with individuals, and help them to find the correct pathway to success, in however this may present itself in their world, and within their capabilities, taking into account their difficulties, barriers and restrictions that cannot be overcome. We do not scoff at blind people, and tell them to stop being stupid and see, as equally we do not get frustrated at wheelchair bound individuals and tell them to perform tasks that require a fully functional able body – we learn more about their difficulties and we approach them from very different angles, appreciating their very obvious barriers to achieve, thus we must very simply use this method with 'hidden' difficulties and 'unfathomable' behaviours, not wasting our time asking why they perform as they do, but 'how can we change to help them'.

I hope you have enjoyed this book and its strategies and methods. I hope you feel empowered to progress and change your approach to the young people you are involved with, and I hope that you keep it as your 'manual' for access when you need to remind yourself about a particular strategy or young person that needs inventive intervention.

Good luck, and I look forward to hearing your successes and new found strategies very soon.